FROM CHAOS TO CALM: A S
TO DECLUTTERING YOUR HOME AND MIND

# THE
# deeCLUTTERED
## EFFECT

# DENISE CLIFFORD

ISBN: 978-1-960136-05-3

# Table of Contents

# Introduction

If your goal is to get your space in order, and you've picked up this book because you're looking for a tool to help give you guidance, motivation, and the confidence to get it done, then thank you for taking a chance with me, and congratulations on taking this first step. My best advice to you, and how to get the most out of this book, is to read it in its entirety before getting started.

I know that may be a tall order. And I know that, for a lot of people, once they have an idea in their head, and the confidence to get started, even if they're not armed with all the right tools, they are ready and eager to dive in.

But much like when you're trying a new recipe or building some IKEA furniture, it's so important to get an understanding of all the steps before you begin. With a recipe, reading it all the way through gives you insight into the ingredients and equipment you need, how to prepare the ingredients, the order you need to complete the steps, and how much time it will take you. I'd like to believe the same goes for reading this book.

I have set this book up into what's essentially three sections. At the very least, do yourself a favor, and take the time to read the first section: chapters two and three, before trying to tackle any area in your home. In chapter two, I address questions frequently asked by my clients and the points I go over with them before getting started. In chapter three I lay out, in detail, my eleven-step process to getting *DeeCluttered*.

In the next section of the book, I address the areas of the home that cause the most challenges and confusion for people when trying to get organized. Each chapter represents one room or area.

The final section is a highlight of some of my favorite pieces of advice. It begins with insights that I share with clients, and really anyone who will listen, followed by tips on how to maintain your organized space, and a recap of my favorite products outlined in the book.

There will be repetition of steps, tenets, tips, and even product recommendations (a lot of the best products are multi-purpose and can be used in a variety of areas). And because getting organized is unique to every person and every home, as I discuss throughout this book, you may find that advice I give on one specific area of the home, speaks to you but applies, in your case, to a different area entirely.

Regardless of how you choose to approach this book, just know that the steps are practical, the philosophy applies to every area of the home, my approach is straight forward with an attempt at some humor, and the results are impactful. Congratulations again, and let's get started.

# CHAPTER 1:

## Picking Up the Pieces

I've heard countless stories about how organizers started in their careers, how it's in their DNA—they were born with a gift, usually OCD—but I find there is a deeper story behind why we are organized or not. My story is even deeper still. I'd like to share my story about the one event in my family's history that changed it all for me and help shape who I am today. It's what my family and I, to this day, simply refer to as "The Accident." But first a little background on how we got there.

I am a child of the 80s. I grew up in a home with my parents and my older brother and sister in Tenafly, NJ. My mother, the oldest of 11, immigrated from the Philippines as a nursing student in 1966 when she was 21 and never left. My father is Italian, born and raised with his younger sister in Brooklyn, NY and had migrated to Long Island when he met my mother. In 1970, they went on a blind date in NYC. My father loves to tell the story of how on their second date, she invited him over to her air-conditioned apartment in Manhattan, and as they watched game 5 of the NBA Championship on her cable TV, where the New York Knicks took on the LA Lakers, she served him a beautiful lobster dinner. The game went into overtime, and apparently was a real nail-biter. As a side note, my father can still recite every detail of this game and the following two games in which the Knicks won the whole thing. After that glorious date, he said to himself, "I am marrying this woman!" And sure enough, six months later, they said "I do." They moved to the suburbs of NJ and in a few years when my mother found out she was pregnant, her mother (and my grandma) moved from the Philippines to help. My grandma stayed until I was about 12 or so, to help raise us. She would periodically take trips back and forth to the Philippines, and then eventually moved between California and Virginia to help raise my cousins. Shortly after my grandma arrived, my mother gave birth to my brother, followed by my sister a year later, and then a few years after had me. Like so many other Filipinos who went into nursing, my mother spent much of her career in various positions as a nurse and health inspector. For the years surrounding my birth, she was working as a supervisor at a nursing home in New York.

While I never gave much thought as to why so many of my aunties, uncles, and cousins are also nurses, I recently learned that there are many factors that have shaped the U.S.-Philippines relationship with nursing. Here's a little bit of a history lesson for you:

> According to a Time Magazine article, the relationship dates back to 1898 when the U.S. bought the Philippines from Spain as part of the Treaty of Paris. The times surrounding the Spanish-American war was a period when there were few medical hospitals and clinics in the region. In response, the U.S. established westernized nursing schools and medical systems. And in 1903, under President Teddy Roosevelt, the Pensionado Act was passed, which offered Filipinos subsidized education and training in medicine. Almost 50 years later, in 1948, under President Harry Truman, the Exchange Visitor Program was established and enabled travel, temporary study, and work experience in the US for Filipinos, but only allowed participants to stay in the country for a maximum of two years. Then in 1965, under President Lyndon B. Johnson, the Immigration Nationality Act granted migrant nurses the opportunity to stay in the country permanently. Because Filipino exchange nurses had been trained in an Americanized nursing system and were fluent in English (due to American colonial education), they were sought out by U.S. hospitals. Since the 1960s, over 150,000 Filipino nurses migrated to the United States, my mother included. Without Filipino nurses, the U.S. healthcare system would have suffered through labor shortages and epidemics, and it would definitely not be what it is today. The history of the international relationship goes even further and is a complicated

story filled with controversy, corruption, discrimination, and exploitation. But it is also a story of opportunity, hope, progress, and freedom. I wear my mom's history like a badge of honor, and I'm so proud of her and all she sacrificed for us. Pretty interesting, right?

My mom is not only a wife and mother of three, but worked as a full-time nurse, and an entrepreneur (she had started many of her own small businesses over the years). My father worked as the CFO of a non-profit organization in New York City, was a volunteer in the Peace Corp, and spent his career as a civil servant. On top of their full-time jobs, our parents still did everything to give us what was a very blessed and memorable childhood despite a major tragedy. They made sure my siblings and I had every opportunity they could provide, they got us to all of our practices, meets, and games on time, and even coached my brother and sister for years. We were involved in a multitude of sports, dance, martial arts, music lessons, and enrichment classes, and attended church every Sunday. My parents were also very involved and active members of the community: HSA/PTA, boosters, Little League, and Lions Clubs. My parents even played on an adult co-ed softball team together, and we would go to the games as a family. My siblings and I would cheer them on, or play "running bases" with the other children of the team. Even before I was born, our family would spend our summers between the local swim club and visiting family. We would devote two weeks every summer down in Virginia Beach to visit my mother's nine younger siblings and their families (my tenth uncle lived in California, so we didn't see them that often). We would take trips around Christmas to visit my father's sister and her family in Minnesota. And throughout the year we would take trips to visit the rest of our extended family across the states.

My father worked long hours and would commute to the big city every day with my great Aunt Lollie from Connecticut, who would spend some of her weekdays with us to make the trek into the city a little easier. In the mornings my mother would commute by car to her job, and my father and aunt would drop us off at preschool, park their car at the Early Learning Center parking lot in Teaneck, and then cross the street to take the bus into New York.

I remember my siblings and I were playing in our living room on a very dark and rainy night in November of 1985 when I was only four years old. At one point, I remember my mother yelling frantically to get us into our blue Honda hatchback. We were children, so we didn't want to stop what we were doing, but there was something in her tone that made us drop our toys. We were quickly shuffled out into the rain and into the back seat of our two-door car. When my mother realized what she was doing, she quickly ushered us right back out and over to our neighbor's house.

I was excited to go over there and play, but I didn't know that our lives were going to be changed forever. That is all I remember of that night. We found out later that my father and aunt were hit by a car in a horrible hit-and-run accident. They were both struck at high speed, thrown, and left there in the rain. Before long, they were each put into separate ambulances. And then the unthinkable happened, my father's ambulance caught on fire. Seeing as my father was in more serious condition, the paramedics immediately called my aunt's ambulance back, and in the pouring rain, switched the stretchers, and rushed my father to the hospital.

That accident left him in a coma for three weeks. And he didn't come home from the hospital until late January of the following year. My mother, God bless her, had to pick up the pieces. Before I get into it, I have to say that my parents are two of the most amazing people I have ever met, and I am so proud of that and of them. Imagine being a 40-year-old man—hell, I'm in my 40s now and I couldn't even imagine this—waking up in a hospital bed, not knowing who you are, where you are, learning that you have a family, and realizing you have to learn how to walk and talk again. Imagine being that man's wife having to explain to the man you love who you and your children are and that everything is going to be okay. Imagine raising three small children and telling them that their Daddy is going to get better, that the ramp you are going to build to get the wheelchair into the house is temporary, that the construction to build a master bedroom on the first floor will not last long, and that Daddy will be okay. The strength my mother had to pick up the pieces without hesitation, and the resilience and dedication my father had to have for his recovery, getting back on his feet, back to work, and back to the life that would become our new normal, still blows my mind to this day.

In my experience, I've found that most married couples who call and need my services are comprised of one who is a bit more organized than the other. Don't get me wrong, sometimes both parties are clutter prone, but usually, one person has a bit of a leg up on their spouse. And it is no different with my family. And you guessed it—my father is the more organized one. Mom, not so much. So, in the days and years that followed my dad's accident, home organization wasn't exactly a priority. To make matters worse, the house I grew up in was built in the 1920s. Closet space, extra storage, walk-in pantries, and mud rooms were not common. They relied more on things like coat racks and armoires for storage. So naturally, like so many of my clients today, if we were not creative with how we used the space, items that belong in cabinets tended to get stacked in closets or stuffed in cabinets, or wherever they could fit.

As the youngest of the three, I didn't really understand the magnitude of the accident or recognize the recovery and footprint that would forever be a part of my father's and our lives. But I knew that things had changed, and I was so little, so I couldn't do much. But I am a people pleaser, and even at such a young age I did what I could through my desire for tidy spaces. From as far back as I can remember, I have always had a natural love for categorizing my toys, books, Halloween candy, and clothes. I categorized, organized, and made little homes for everything I owned. I used old shoe boxes or bins to corral all my little tchotchkes, notes from my friends in class, my little treasures, and my collections. I even made a huge photo album of all the Bar and Bat Mitzvah invitations I received over the years.

So, when I realized I could take my little tendencies outside of my bedroom, and apply them to the rest of the house, I knew it would help my family tremendously. When I saw the positive impact being organized had on my parents' lives, their attitude, and their happiness, I did it every chance I could. And I mean a lot. As I got older, my skills got better. I re-categorized the pantry by taking everything out, getting rid of expired foods, cleaning the surfaces, and putting everything back in a more organized manner. I organized the drawers the same way by taking out all the items, getting rid of duplicates, relocating things to their proper place, wiping the surfaces, and putting everything back in an organized way. I'd clean any space that became a dumping ground, became cluttered with stuff, or became an afterthought. I was picking up the pieces, just like my mom was.

And that's where it all began. Add that desire to please my parents, and to help my brother or sister when they wanted to have friends over, coupled with my love for categorizing, and my love for math and you've got one motivated child. (That's right, math. I went to Kumon, I love Tetris, I am a closet nerd… I love the symmetry and figuring out how to fit pieces together like a puzzle.) Who knew that my childhood trauma, a people pleasing character, and a nerdy personality would be a recipe for a career?

Naturally, when I went to college and lived in a shared space the size of a shoebox, keeping organized and clutter free was so important to me. It was already ingrained. My college roommate, Michele, even called me Monica (for those of you that don't know, she was one of the six leads on Friends, an overly controlling neat freak with OCD). What's even more comical, is one day while we were laughing about my Monica-tendencies, for shits and giggles I actually counted, and I too have 11 categories of towels.

As I was saying—every living space thereafter was always a fun challenge for me. I loved figuring out how to keep it organized, functional, and efficient.

Then it got to a point where I started organizing my family's and friends' pantries, closets, and junk drawers because it would only take me a few minutes to make big changes. Things that seem so logical to me are a mystery to others, and it amazed me that they didn't see it the way that I did. And I love that. I get such a kick out of bringing joy to people by simply showing them how easy it is to set up their space where they can see everything, access everything, and where everything has a home. I love seeing how happy and how relieved they become by doing something that I find relatively easy and that comes so naturally to me. As word started to get around with friends and now even my extended family that I loved doing this, that it was quick and easy for me, my business began. And even now, it's not uncommon for me to be hanging out in the kitchen with my girlfriends while attending a party at one of their homes, and low-key emptying, sorting, and decluttering the Tupperware drawer.

Today I live in Fairfield, NJ with my husband and two small children, and while our home is very organized, trying to keep up with the hectic schedules of four people, juggling school, work, home, and all that's in between, gets challenging. So, you can imagine I know what it is like to feel overwhelmed and trapped by the abundance of stuff in and around your home. I've been there. And I've seen the other side.

I don't need to explain that living a life of clutter can cloud your physical space and mind. But what you may not know is that life becomes easier when your home is in order. Every day you will feel less stressed and regain the time and energy to do the things you used to do or have been wanting to do. And, you will have pride in your home—a feeling that maybe you didn't have before.

Over the years, I have read countless books, articles, blogs, watched endless tutorials and videos, taken courses, spoken with experts all in an effort to immerse myself into the world of organizing. I've done all of this, so that you don't have to. With this book, I hope I can provide some practical tips and tricks that I've learned along the way; tips I've shared with countless families to help them gain back control of their space, their mind, and their lives. And I hope that it does the same for you.

# CHAPTER 2:

## Getting Started: and Frequently Asked Questions

---

*"The stuff you own ends up owning you." – Tyler Durden*

---

I geek out when I start day one on a job because I know that while my clients are so excited to get started and know they will be so happy once their space is organized, they *usually don't know* just how big the impact on their lives is going to be. I'm talking physically, mentally, emotionally, and financially. Because whether we realize it or not, our environment seriously affects our lives. It can influence our moods, cause frustration, anxiety, and make us feel overwhelmed. Being disorganized wastes time and money, and it can affect how we interact in our relationships, and how we carry about our day.

We live in a fast-paced world, and sometimes the thing that slows us down is the stress that comes from all that clutter. Sometimes, it's the actual clutter. So it goes without saying, that a life with less clutter is a life with less stress. We are all familiar with frantically pacing from room to room in a panic, not being able to find that *one thing* you need. When you know exactly where everything is, you can move quickly if you need to, not because you have to. Instead of stressing about the mess, we can relax and focus our time on more important things.

Getting organized will do more than create more space in your home. It will improve your mind and body, not just your physical space. It will promote positive mental health, give you more energy, and provide better sleep. You'll regain control of your life, get back valuable time, and avoid wasting money! Think of all the time you spent thinking about a lost item, the time you wasted looking for something you misplaced, or the money you have thrown away replacing items you already own. It all adds up!

I'm so excited for you. Whether you are getting ready for seasonal events, like the start of a school year, birthdays, or the holidays, when our homes are naturally bombarded with more stuff or you are experiencing a major life event, a new home, marriage, divorce, a new baby, or you are simply ready to make some changes, getting organized will help you in countless ways. While it's easy to be intimidated or overwhelmed when you're staring at a room that looks like a bomb just went off, I hope this book will help guide you through the process with practical advice and tips on how to avoid the pitfalls of being disorganized.

## Your BASELINE

Clutter of the space leads to clutter of the mind. People's ideas of what is cluttered, clean, messy, organized, or disorganized differ. Understandably, our goals in getting organized will also differ. Regardless of what your views or goals are, the bottom line is usually the same.

Getting organized is about knowing where your things are and being able to access them easily. Getting decluttered is about creating smart and sustainable systems to make your life easier! I like to call my goal with my clients getting to your "*baseline.*" The baseline is the vision you have for your space, your goal, and a future reference point that you and your family will strive to maintain every day, especially on those days when you get a little off track. It will happen. But having that baseline makes it easier to stay decluttered.

---

*"That's your HOME!! Are you too good for your home?"*
*– Happy Gilmore*

---

One of my strongest beliefs is that EVERYTHING SHOULD HAVE A HOME. You should be able to instruct or direct anyone in your family to where something can be found. Eventually, you shouldn't even need to instruct anyone, because they will just know. Homes should be logical and almost obvious. More on this later.

Think of the time you'll save when you don't have to stop what you're doing to go and get it yourself because it's clear to everyone. No more, "Honey, where is the..?" "Mommy, I can't find my…" If you make sure everything has a home and hold people (including yourself) accountable for putting everything back in that home, you should be able to find things easily, clean up faster, and encourage independence for your family.

So, like I do with all my clients, I will address the most common concerns before we get started:

## Where Should I Start First?

This is a question I hear so often. You want to think about that number one spot that's driving you crazy. I'm talking about that space that *really* trips you up, delays you, and causes audible frustration. It's the spot that gives you anxiety just thinking about, somewhere that slows you down when trying to start your day. We will refer to this type of area as your "Hot Spot." While everyone's Hot Spot is different, in my experience, these places are usually somewhere in the kitchen, the closet, or the garage.

Get out a pad of paper and whatever your Hot Spot is, write it down and star it. Then think about what other areas there are. Your next task is to create a list of areas you know could use some TLC. Take a walk around your home and begin to list all the projects big or small that you'd like to tackle.

Categorize your list into big vs. small projects. The big projects are those that you are going to need to devote some significant time to, but the small ones can be tackled by carving out an hour or so (maybe even less.) Prioritize your list and make sure you are ranking the most important areas at the top. Keep in mind there can be a difference between what is the "most important" area versus the "messiest" area. In some cases, they are not the same. The best way to differentiate these two is to determine what area your day-to-day will benefit the most by being organized. These are the areas that cause you the most frustration, stress, and delays in being productive and efficient with your time.

For example, your garage may be the messiest space, but if the disorganization of your master closet makes getting dressed a nightmare, causes delays getting out of the door every day, and produces physical pain and stress when you are winding down at night, then this space is definitely more important. Now, you may still want to include your garage on your list, but it may not be sitting at the top of most important priorities. That's why I find it so helpful to keep an ongoing list.

I'm very fortunate to have a cleaning lady, (we didn't have one growing up.) But truth be told, I'm one of those people who likes to tidy up before she comes. My husband just laughs and thinks it's ridiculous. C'est la vie. But sometimes, that glorious day when she arrives creeps up on me, and I am short on time and left scrambling to clear off some of the dresser tops or tabletops that have accumulated clutter since her last visit. So, what do I do? I pile up the paperwork, or whatever the clutter may be, and I stuff it into one of two drawers. But I don't leave it there to be forgotten; I add it to my ongoing list of items that need decluttering or organizing. That's right, I'm a professional organizer and I still have spots in my home that need organization or just some occasional zhuzhing. But I keep a list because it makes me feel like I'm not forgetting anything—like those piles of clutter to go through—and it gives me more control over my space and my belongings. It definitely helps keep my stress levels down. I highly recommend.

Usually, the most important or crucial areas to organize will take some time and focused energy. We will dive into specifics in later chapters with detailed tips on each room, time needed, and where to start.

## How Much Time Do I Need?

*"By all means, move at a glacial pace, you know how that thrills me." – Miranda Priesley*

Set aside the time on a weekend or day that you know will not be interrupted.

Whatever time you can allocate for your first project, one to two hours or even more, make sure that you can focus: free from distractions and interruptions. Say no to the Sunday brunch invite, take a break from the laundry, send the children to Grandma's... whatever you need to do to ensure you are truly devoting your undivided attention to your project.

Below is a rough estimate of about how much time it will take to declutter an area in your home:

| Time Needed to Get Organized | |
|---|---|
| Area | Hours |
| Closet | 4 - 6 |
| Bedroom | 4 - 6 |
| Kitchen | 6 - 8 |
| Children's Area | 6 - 8 |
| Garage | 8 - 12 |
| Office | 6+ (depending on paperwork) |
| Basement or Attic | 12-20 |

You should adjust accordingly based on certain factors like how much inventory you have, or how big or small your space is. These estimates are based on a general assumption that a cluttered space of about 4' wide by 2' deep would take approximately two to four hours to complete. If you know you have a huge wardrobe, tons of pantry items, or endless toys to go through, make sure you add some time to these estimates. Also factor in how much time per day you can devote to your project. Most often, if you can set aside larger chunks of time, let's say a weekend with three hours each day, you will most likely get more accomplished than if you set aside one hour each day for six days.

Once you've tackled your biggest priorities and your Hot Spot(s), trying to determine what project to move on to can be challenging. I always advise getting little wins wherever you can.

You can complete smaller projects (like junk drawers, medicine cabinets, mail, or gift bags) fairly quickly. And yes, I said gift bags. We all know that person—could be you, is definitely me—who holds on to too many gift bags and boxes to reuse, and we know that those bags of bags are disorganized, and seldom actually put into action.

Examples of smaller projects include—but are not limited to:

- Junk drawer
- Mail center (or a command center)
- Medicine cabinets
- Makeup drawer/makeup collection
- Sock drawer (we'll discuss mine later)
- Wallet or purse
- Nightstand
- Bathroom vanity drawer
- Cleaning out expired items from your refrigerator
- Cleaning out your email
- Organizing the photos on your phone
- Deleting old apps from your phone

The more you get a taste of that feeling of accomplishment and relief, the more motivated you will be to continue. And hey, if you're really quick to get one of these smaller areas completed, consider tackling more than one. As you continue your home organization journey, you will begin to understand how quickly or slowly you tend to work and get things done. You will get better, faster, and more confident with each space you conquer!

## What Items Should I Buy to Get My (Fill in the Blank) Organized?

NOTHING! There are no cookie-cutter answers or solutions to organizing people's homes. And you shouldn't make any purchases without going through the steps of getting decluttered first.

My biggest challenge is when a client says, "I went and got all these bins!"

No! Don't do it; don't go and spend money on products you don't know you'll need. As I explain in the following chapters, there is a definite method to this process. There is no sense in wasting money on baskets or bins without going through the steps. Because you don't know what you don't know, until you know it.

Plus, you may find that you can use items or storage pieces that you already have around the house. What a way to save money! I always try to incorporate baskets, bins, or cute boxes that my clients already own. And, if you don't waste your money on those bins that usually end up being less functional than you hoped, you'll have more money to spend on some quality storage solutions that will stand the test of time.

## Do I Have to Spend a Fortune to Get My Home Organized?

Absolutely not. You can definitely go through the steps to get decluttered without going out and spending hundreds if not thousands of dollars on plastic bins and top of the line storage. Some of the tips and tricks I provide in the chapters ahead offer solutions using items you already have in your home, or inexpensive alternatives to some of the pricier options out there. You can have big transformations on a small budget!

Don't be intimidated by The Container Store! I hear all the time how people are overwhelmed when they walk in or how everything is too expensive there, but they are completely misguided. I suggest working with the staff, they are all very well trained and can show you a variety of options. They offer a wide selection of price points based on size and materials to fit all of your storage needs. You can also search your local off-price retailers like Home Goods or World Market. Amazon has a lot of wonderful and affordable options and a lot of designer dupes, as does Target and Walmart. I've also sourced some creative solutions from Home Depot for the garage or Staples for the office. There are endless options.

## Are There Any Products You Recommend to All of Your Clients?

Yes, unless you are vertically blessed, I always recommend a step stool, and in a perfect world, one for every area of your home where you are struggling to reach the top shelf. I'm only 5'5" and ¾. Yes, I hold onto that ¾ like my life depends on it. To be honest, I think a doctor at some point in my youth told me this number, and I refuse to let that ¾ go. As I was saying, I'm not as vertically challenged as a lot of people, but I still struggle to reach the top shelf in my kitchen, garage, pantry, linen closet, master closet, and children's closets. Pretty much, all over my house. So you guessed it, I have a step stool in each of those locations. Some are shorter than others, some are sturdier than others depending on the space and what I'm retrieving and depending on the distance I'm trying to make up.

Now, this is not a directive to be excessive (like me) and get one for each room, just know that having one close to those areas that you need it in will save you extra time and help foster that easy access we are seeking.

Do your research when determining which step stool to purchase. They are all relatively inexpensive and come in a variety of shapes, colors, and sizes.

## Do I Need to *DeeClutter* My Entire Home to Get Started?

This is a somewhat controversial topic. Some people feel it's critical to declutter every room in your home before getting started or going out and making your purchases. The rationale is that you get an opportunity to see if there are storage bins on hand that you can repurpose or items in a different location that belong in the area you are tackling.

For example, you may have some unused baskets in the garage that would work perfectly in the pantry; or you may have an assortment of writing supplies stored in your bedroom that belong in the office.

While I agree with the philosophy to some extent, I don't believe it's necessary for everyone. If you have the time to declutter thoroughly throughout your entire home, then more power to you. But I know that my clients, and myself included, do not have the time or patience to declutter an entire home in one shot.

I recommend starting with one project at a time. Do not make the mistake of taking too much on at once. You will become overwhelmed and get discouraged. Getting organized is one of those, "It has to get worse before it gets better," things, so I highly recommend completing one project before moving onto the next one. And that is how we will approach your journey in this book.

What is important, however, is making sure that you gather all the items that are supposed to go in whatever room or space you are tackling. For example: if you know you have wrapping paper in your garage, your dining room, and your bedroom but are working to organize your gifting area, make sure you go around and gather all those items. Or, if you are getting your playroom in order, gather all the toys that are scattered throughout the house. This doesn't include if you have two storage places for an item (like backstock or double sets for convenience—I will share my method on having three sets of scotch tape later in the book).

I also suggest making sure that all your inventory is accounted for. For example, if you are organizing your closet, make sure your laundry is done and out of the laundry room. If you are organizing your kitchen, I suggest you stock your pantry before starting the process. As I mention in future chapters, it's important to understand all that you own. How else will you know if you have enough room for it or how to organize it properly?

## What Do I Do if I Have Trouble Letting Go?

Getting organized is different than tidying up or putting things away. To truly make your space functional, you really have to sort and edit your possessions.

Now, I'm not a huge advocate of throwing everything away. I get it; I am a sentimental person, so I know about holding onto memories. And I have a love for fashion. I know it's cyclical and that things always come back into style, and I love the idea of saving some of my designer pieces for my daughter. So, I know all about jammed closets and drawers that don't close.

Even my husband refuses to let go of certain clothes. What is it with men and holding on to old basketball jerseys? You know you're never going to wear them again! And the junk drawer of old key chains? I've seen it over and over. But I don't judge, and I don't urge people to throw everything away. It's not about getting rid of your possessions; it's about organizing them to fit your lifestyle and daily habits.

Decluttering and getting organized is not a one-size-fits-all type of world. Because you are going to create zones based on the physical layout of your space, your habits, and your MF'ers, no project is identical. Your MF'ers are your most frequently used items… or Most Frequents (not what you were thinking).

I will recommend some of my favorite products, and some of the common places for certain categories, but your decluttering journey will be unique. What will be the same, regardless of your space, style or daily routine, is that everything will have a home. Everything, for the most part, should be visible; if it's not, then you should know that it's there (hint hint—use a label).

My philosophy is: if you truly use it, if you have the space for it, and if you can put it away neatly and functionally, then keep it. If you're struggling to close a drawer, or items are falling out of a cabinet because there's just too much stuff, then it's time to assess what needs to go to give you the space you need.

There are a few tricks for decluttering the three areas that usually cause the most stress:

**Everyday clutter, clothes, and sentimental items.**

**Everyday Clutter:**

For everyday areas (like the junk drawer or medicine cabinet) or everyday items (like kitchen utensils and office supplies): *use the 20/20 rule.*

The 20/20 Rule for decluttering can be traced back to Joshua Fields Milburn and Ryan Nicodemus of "The Minimalists." Simply put, if you are struggling to decide whether to keep an item "just in case" you'll need it, ask yourself two questions:

Can the item be replaced in 20 minutes or less? (That means driving down the road to your local pharmacy or hardware store.) Can it be replaced for $20 or less? If the answer is yes to both, then it's time to let it go. If it's yes to one, then take a deep breath and really consider whether the item is worth keeping. Is the extra clutter worth it?

Because there is no sense in keeping an item "just in case" if you can't find it when you need it.

You'll often find yourself confident in your decision to part ways with that coffee grinder you never use. And that's what this theory does; it helps give you confidence and comfort in your decision to let go of those smaller, often inexpensive items that tend to take up so much space.

Now, this rule does not apply to every item or area you may be decluttering, but it does help speed up the decision process for those everyday things that most likely create the bulk of your clutter. These fast and impressive results can also help spark an impetus to move on to a bigger, and usually, more intimidating category.

**Clothes:**

For clothes, we review the categories and process in more detail in Chapter 4. But when you struggle to let clothing go, you will need to ask yourself a few questions:

- Do you love it?
- Do you wear it?
- Would you buy it again?
- Does it fit?
- Is it in good condition?
- Are you really going to repair or get it altered?
- Does it project the image you want to portray?

**Sentimental Items:**

Sentimental items can be tricky. I am a very sentimental person, and as I mentioned I do not believe in throwing everything away (which is code for I have a lot of memento boxes) AS LONG AS THERE IS A HOME FOR IT. And because our sentimental items are so, well, sentimental, they need *special* homes. Whether it's a weatherproof bin, a beautiful keepsake box, or a leather storage case, there is a container out there for everything.

And if you are holding onto these items because they mean something to you, you should take care of them. Whether you have piles of greeting cards that you have saved over the years, or your child has all the martial arts belts they earned, or a jar of shells you collected from all the beach vacations you went on, or a box of key chains from your travels, whatever your mementos are— as long as you have the room to store it properly, in a place that is *not taking up prime real-estate* (think the top of your closet, attic, or basement) then I say keep it! Prime Real Estate is the area, the cabinets, shelves, or drawers that are front and center with the most visibility and access. Coveted space!

When my clients are on the fence about keeping something that "kiiiinda" has some sentimental value, I ask if other items, photographs, or videos hold a stronger value of that memory. Usually there is, and if there is, then there is more confidence in their decision to let that something go. If there is still confusion or hesitation, I suggest taking a picture of it. Sometimes, we don't want to forget the idea or vision of something, so we hold onto tchotchkes and clutter our space when really, a picture will suffice.

Just keep in mind that in some cases, you need to treat your sentimental items as a separate project. If you keep these keepsake items in a dresser drawer or a box under your bed, do not incorporate those items into, let's say, *DeeCluttering* your bedroom closet.

Stay focused on the project on your list and set aside some time for reminiscing and going through those sentimental items at a later time. And when you do, organize along the way. Why else do we keep them, but to actually enjoy holding, touching, seeing them, and remembering them properly? Getting sucked into a wormhole of old keepsakes and strolling down memory lane can be a huge time suck for your *DeeCluttering* process. But it happens to all of us. Embrace the time suck and go down memory lane, just make sure to set aside the time for it.

Now that you have your list of areas that you want to focus on, you've picked out the top priorities and set aside the time, take a deep breath, be proud of yourself for taking the first step, and get ready to start. Our next step is to review the process which can be applied to every area of your home.

As you go through the steps outlined in the next chapters, you will begin to see the results and feel the physical impact getting decluttered gives you. You'll not only feel a sense of relief, but you will also gain the confidence to take on more.

# CHAPTER 3:
## Overall Process

The best way to make sure that your organizational systems work and last, is to make them functional and beautiful. If your new layout helps you save time *and* you love the way it looks, it makes it easier for you to want to keep it that way.

The key is simple, uncomplicated systems that fit your habits, tendencies, and lifestyle. You will need to do some honest self-reflection about **how you *want* to use** your space versus **how you *actually* use** your space.

For example, you may have dreams of being a baker. You bought all the supplies and tools, and they sit front and center in your pantry. But you just don't bake. If you're like me, the candy cane cookies you tried to make for your daughter's first-grade holiday party turned into little blobs resembling a deranged snowman. Now I'm not saying to throw away those dreams or supplies, I'm just saying it's probably best to put these tools in a less prominent space and avoid assigning prime real estate to something seasonal or barely used.

Everything should have a home, and every home should have a category assigned to it—even if that category is *"Room to Grow."*

> I love to leave room for clients to grow into. We all know we will continue accumulating more stuff (especially those with growing children). But too much empty, undesignated space leaves room for clutter and tends to turn into dumping grounds for random stuff.

**Denise Clifford** ✓
@dee.cluttered

Before you get started, do us both a favor: TAKE A PICTURE! There is nothing more satisfying than a great before and after picture or video to document the transformation.

You can even take some mid-DeeCluttering progress photos. Then upload and tag your pictures on Instagram, Facebook or TikTok with #igotdeecluttered and share your journey and your finished project with me and my team!

We're ripping off the band-aid and diving right in.

### Supplies to Get Started:

I always start with a large flat surface, a box of garbage bags, a variety of different-sized containers, a packet of Post-Its or masking tape for labeling, and a Sharpie marker.

### For your surface:

Whether it's a folding table, a bed, or a kitchen table, make sure you have enough surface area to work on. You usually need more space than you think.

### Garbage bags:

Even if you feel like "There really isn't any garbage in this room, it's all things I want to keep," you will be mistaken. There is, without a doubt, always garbage.

**Pro Tip:** When organizing your closet: if your closet rods are high, or you have a lot of clothing to go through, I love to use a rolling rack to make changing over hangers and reviewing hanging clothes easier on the back and shoulders. Not everyone has a rolling rack at their fingertips, so just remember this is not necessary. Even a folding table or waist-high surface for folding clothes is better for you to use than the floor or a low bed.

**Containers:**

You can use anything you have around the house as your containers: shopping bags, old shoe boxes, any bins, or even empty Amazon boxes that haven't been recycled. You will use these as temporary homes, let's call them *vacation rentals*, for your things while your categories develop.

**Post-Its:**

They will be a godsend (you can even use masking tape and a Sharpie). It's really important to put Post-Its on your containers, especially if you're using opaque boxes or bins. Just don't get those Post-Its that are stuck together like an accordion, they are the worst, and I'm always writing upside down and waste a million of them and end the day with a pile of crumpled Post-It notes in my pocket. Avoid at all costs.

**Step 1: Sort**

Now, it's time to take out all the contents. In this step, you will clear things out one by one. (Refer to chapter two to determine where to start.)

To really understand the size of your space, as well as the amount of inventory you have, it's best to get EVERYTHING OUT. Yes, I mean EVERYTHING. By having a clean slate, you're able to grasp the true scope of whatever space you're organizing and get the chance to really re-imagine the area.

---

*"Don't feel overwhelmed. Just do one thing at a time."*
*– Sue Ellen Crandall*

---

As you clear each item out one by one, you are going to sort and categorize items into piles separated by categories based on type, color, season, etc. (You can refer to the room-specific chapters ahead to help guide you in common categories if you are having trouble.) Your categories can be whatever you want them to be. I even use categories such as: "for (hubby) to review" or "soft fuzzy socks to wear around the house."

Group similar items. Your categories may start out very broad. As you take out more items, your categories will naturally become more specific. Soon you'll begin to see how much of each item you may have.

Some spaces will lend themselves to general categories (think "Cleaning Products" under a kitchen sink) while other spaces may need to be drilled down to more specific categories (think "Cough & Cold" vs. "Pain & Digestion" products in a bathroom medicine cabinet).

If you're in the kitchen you may find 15 spatulas, in the garage you may have 35 Allen wrenches, or let's say in the laundry room you may have 75 cleaning cloths—all true stories. Not only will this give you the opportunity to let go of some of the excess you're carrying, but it will also give you an idea of what type of bins and storage solutions you'll need.

If you have a lot of little things, you know you'll need a few smaller containers. Are there a lot of larger appliances or tools? Then you will need bigger baskets or bins, or you may need to make sure you leave open shelf space for these items (because not everything needs to or should be in a bin).

If you don't know where to start, grab the first thing in front of you. Determine the item's category, set it down, and pick up the next item. And just keep going.

DON'T FORGET TO USE POST-IT NOTES! It will make the whole process easier and remind you what category you have in front of you. Even as a professional, I forget what certain categories I've designated, and the use of Post-It notes helps make it clear what everything is. It will save you time, and you can avoid the frustration of trying to rack your brain for what is what!

### Step 2: Discard, Donate, Relocate

As you are sorting your categories, you will keep the items you love and that you actually use. Simultaneously, you want to pull out anything that no longer serves a purpose, or that belongs in another room. You will begin to create three additional piles:

Discard, Donate, and Relocate

**THIS IS VERY IMPORTANT.** In order to get organized, you must recognize that a critical and necessary step when you declutter is **letting go of some of your items.** There is no sense in organizing things that you don't need or use. It is a waste of time, money, and energy. Trust the process.

**Discard:**

Have a garbage bag designated for discard. Let go of anything broken, damaged/stained beyond repair, or used up.

**Donate:**

Items that are gently used and still in good condition. Think of it as something you or someone in need would happily take if given the opportunity. Don't forget to label your donation pile.

---

*"Give it away, give it away, give it away now"*
*– Red Hot Chili Peppers*

---

When it comes to donations, we all have great intentions for the drop-off, but for some reason, it's pretty popular to drive around with a big old bag in our trunk for weeks or keep a pile of donations in our garage for months. Do a quick search online for local spots that take donations.

- GreenDrop. They accept donations on behalf of one of their partner charities (Purple Heart, American Red Cross, and National Federation of the Blind to name a few). You can schedule a pick-up or drop off at one of their locations (and you don't even have to get out of your vehicle).
- The Veterans Association will accept most items and will schedule a home pickup for easy removal.
- The Humane Society is a great resource for used linens, towels, and the like.
- Explore Buy Nothing Groups: The Buy Nothing Project has groups worldwide (you can find them on Facebook or on their own app.)

- Local preschools or daycares are usually happy to take gently used toys or games.
- Your local library generally takes used books.

Do a little research and find what works best for you. A lot of these places will do all the heavy lifting for you and offer receipts for tax deductions. Win-win.

**Relocate:**

This pile will turn into multiple piles when you have items that belong in several rooms. Don't forget to label which area or room these items are going to.

Once you have completed going through every item and you have a clean slate, take a deep breath, and congratulate yourself. That was not easy. And your place probably looks worse than when you started. But take another deep breath, remind yourself it has to get worse before it gets better.

Having the space completely empty is an important step because it will give a real snapshot of how much space you have. Plus, having a clean slate makes it easier to imagine all the possibilities of what your layout can be.

### Step 3: Remove

Once you have gone through all the contents of the space, immediately remove the garbage and the donations and take the "relocate" items to the rooms they belong in. No sense in keeping those items there! Simply clearing out these three categories will give you some relief in physical clutter in the room and give you such a great sense of accomplishment.

**Pro Tip:** One of the worst things you can do is stop or pause midway through the initial sorting process. It's best to get through this first stage so that you're not faced with clutter on whatever surface you're working on. Do your best to get through this step before taking a break or calling it quits for the day. You'll thank me later.

### Step 4: Clean Slate

Whether that means a gentle sweep with a broom or a deep clean with some heavy-duty cleaner and a Mr. Clean Magic Eraser (those things are *magic!*), make sure all the surfaces are clean and dry.

**Step 5: List It**

Now for a little bit of paperwork. Make a list of the categories that you created in step four.

    a. Make sure that your categories have enough items in them to warrant an actual category. If not, ask yourself which of these items can be grouped together to form a larger category, and that can essentially live together in a home.

    b. Determine your MF'ers. You'll want to have these items stored at your fingertips. Mark those MF'ers with a star so you make sure they go in the Prime Real Estate.

Once you have your working list of categories, put each item from that list onto a separate Post-It note to prepare for the next step.

**Step 6: Time For a Stroll**

Walk the space and think about an ideal organizational layout. If the thought of this intimidates you, don't worry. Take a deep breath and think about how you currently use the space. And then think about what your goal or vision for the space is. What works and what doesn't?

Do you want to get dressed more quickly? Do you find yourself walking from one dresser to another dresser when you get dressed for bed because you have pajamas over here, but undergarments over there? Does it make sense to combine those?

Do you want an easier time cooking dinner? Do you sometimes end up burning your meal because your spatulas are so far from the stovetop? Maybe it makes sense to reconfigure all your tools to accommodate your cooking style.

You'll want to factor in a few things as you walk the room and reimagine your space:

**Zones:**

You want to create zones based on how you use the space (i.e., how you get dressed, cook, snack). Zones will create a more functional setup and make it easier to navigate through your space and your belongings.

Now, if you're like so many of my clients, totally overwhelmed and unsure of how you want to use your space, creating zones may be a big challenge.

You can use my _**"Department Store Trick"**_ to determine what categories should be stored together or near each other. And it can apply to any area of your house.

> Organizing the garage? Think about a hardware store.
> Organizing the kitchen? Think about a kitchen and home furnishings store.
> Organizing the pantry? Think about a grocery store.
> Organizing the closet? Think about a department store.
> Organizing the medicine cabinet? Think about a pharmacy.

What are their categories? How are they grouped together? Think about grouping your space into zones similar to how these shops break out their departments. Now we know that many of these places are strategic in their flow and placement of certain departments or zones, so be objective. Like the grocery store: the staples and MF'ers are placed in the back so you have to walk through the entire store to get to them. They do this so you'll buy more. Kind of like a casino, they pump the oxygen and hide the clocks. Those tricksters.

I will provide a list of categories for some areas that cause the most confusion in the chapters ahead.

**Prime Real Estate:**

Don't improperly assign infrequently used categories to the PRIME REAL ESTATE! Make sure you put your MF'ers in these prominent locations for easy access.

**Big items:**

Remember to factor in those large items, i.e., appliances, equipment, large boots, and big coats. You need to consider bigger items that will take up a good portion of real estate and may affect the configuration of your shelves or layout. You don't want to realize in the end that the only place left where the leaf blower will fit is smack in the middle of the garage floor. It usually leads to starting over again. Don't do it.

Once you've walked the space and taken some time to think about what categories belong close to each other and what will work with your flow and physical layout, assign each category to an area by putting the Post-It notes in that space. This will be their "new home." The Post-Its will help ensure you're not missing a category from your "keep" piles and help determine if you have enough real estate for the category. Remember, nothing is permanent, so don't stress if you can't figure out the best configuration right off the bat. In fact, a lot of times, you may live with your new layout and discover that you need to tweak a little bit and maybe do a swap-a-roo. Don't worry.

## Step 7: Desperate Times Call For Desperate Measures

Get out the measuring tape. Measure everything: the length, width, height, and depth of each shelf, cabinet, and closet. Be sure to measure spaces between shelves, and to factor in anything obstructing the space. Think hinges on cabinets, pipes under a sink, heating units or radiators, molding, or baseboards. Write everything down; even consider using graph paper to map out and make a blueprint of the space.

You also want to measure the items that you will be putting into the space to make sure that you are buying containers big enough for everything to fit in.

## Step 8: Detective Work

Research the best storage solutions for your project. Do you need deep drawer bins or dividers? Does the category look better with visible or hidden storage? In the sections ahead, I will give some of my favorite solutions for certain categories and spaces, but feel free to deviate and look further for alternative options. You can take inspiration from anywhere or by using resources like Houzz, Pinterest, Instagram, or TikTok.

If you're at a loss, I suggest doing a little research. "How do I organize my sneakers?" "What's the best way to store batteries?" Simply look online. Google, Pinterest, Instagram, and YouTube are wonderful and useful tools. Type in "Best way to organize my sneakers/batteries." Et voila, a multitude of shoe organizers/battery bins will pop up.

---

*"Get in loser, we're going shopping," – Regina George*

---

**Step 9: Time To Go Shopping**

As far as products go, I love uniformity for categories like hangers or drawer dividers, and in places like the garage or basement storage. You can go complimentary with pantries and closets (think cherry wood and white wire for a pantry or acrylic and fabric boxes for closets). I love the look of having one type of container per shelf in a pantry or cabinet. Think three lazy Susans, or four wire open bins, or a whole shelf of three-tier risers. Just try to keep in the same family, whether your anchor to the palette is black, gray, brown, or white.

With the growth in popularity of home organization, locations to buy solutions are everywhere. Some of my favorites include:

- The Container Store
- Amazon
- Costco
- Home Goods
- Wayfair

- Target
- Home Depot
- WalMart
- Staples
- Ikea

Remember, you can save some money by re-using storage solutions you already have on hand. I love repurposing a cute box or a bin purchased on a Home Goods shopping spree. We all love to save money, and if you get a little creative, you can do just that.

*Always* buy a few extra of everything and even consider a few extra options for a category. You can ensure you have the right storage solutions (and amount) by placing your empty bins or dividers in the space to double-check that everything fits your liking. As you're playing around with the layout, it's always easier when you have more of an item or different options if, let's say, a bin or basket doesn't fit exactly as you imagined. It happens, even to professionals. There's nothing worse than wishing you had a third basket to fill out the space or balance the shelf. Simply return whatever you don't use or hold on to them for another area.

## Step 10: Last Look

Take one last look at your stuff. Review the items you are keeping and ensure you are happy with your selection. Maybe you were on the fence about an item, maybe not.

## Step 11: Finish Line

And finally, put everything away neatly and functionally. We will get into details on storing and folding particular items and optimizing specific dead zones and trouble areas in the following chapters.

A few things to note:

- Determine if you need labels or if it is clear and evident without them. Most of the time, labels elevate a space. Sometimes, I think it does the opposite. They especially help if you share the space with family, a spouse, or roommates by fostering accountability to find and put things back in their home, but they are not always necessary.

  I love my Brother P-Touch Cube. It can make labels of different sizes from ¼ to 2" wide. And when I'm getting really crafty, my Cricut Joy takes the labeling up a notch. There are also several pre-made labels to buy on Etsy or Amazon. My favorites are from The Talented Kitchen. But they are missing a few for me personally, maybe a *DeeCluttered* label line is in my future.

- Once you get started, a great trick is to SET A TIMER! I love to set incremental alarms so I can track my progress and I don't lose track of the time.

Just remember all that clutter didn't accumulate in a day, so don't expect it to disappear in a day!

I remember when I was in my 20s and I hired a personal trainer. I told him that I wanted to work on my core, and I'm not lying, from that point on he only talked to my stomach. It was so strange; he would literally bend down and talk to my gut. Strange tactic, and I'm sure you're not surprised I didn't stay with him for long. But one thing did stick with me from my short stint with him: When I asked him how long it would take me to get rock hard abs, he asked me, "Well how long did it take for you to get a soft belly? Did it take you a week? You're not going to reverse all that in a week." That one hit home.

And it hits home when I tell that to my clients about their clutter. It's going to take time, and it's going to take an adjustment in how you live your life. And if you're serious about getting back the time that having clutter in your life wastes, if you want that sigh of relief that comes with less anxiety by having your space and your mind cleared of the excess stuff, if you want to gain control of your life, then you have to accept that you're going to have to put in some effort. Even if it's little by little, change can happen. I'm going to help give you advice on simple adjustments that will have big impacts.

That's all folks. When you complete these steps, you can say that you have officially been *DeeCluttered*. Enjoy your new space, move to the next item on your list, and repeat steps 1 – 11. Don't lose the momentum to move on to the next area on your list! And don't forget to take a before and after picture!

 Take a picture! #igotdeecluttered

The rest of this book is divided into chapters that represent the main areas of the home. Feel free to jump around or skip chapters entirely if they do not apply or speak to you.

# CHAPTER 4:

## Kitchen

---

*"If you can't take the heat, getchyo' a$$ out the
kitchen…we on a mission" – Coolio*

---

The kitchen is the heart of the home and, unfortunately, can easily and quickly become one of the most disorganized areas. That's why I love starting in the kitchen. It's easy to know when to let go of items (expiration dates) and it's usually pretty apparent when you need to donate something (do you need four vegetable peelers?). As an amateur cook, food lover, and a professional snack maker, I completely understand and appreciate the need for a functional kitchen.

When starting out in your kitchen, remember something my old trainer would say: that Rome wasn't built in a day. While some cabinets or drawers can be decluttered fairly quickly, a project like the kitchen can take hours, and sometimes even a full weekend. Just make sure you're setting aside the time and not stopping in the middle at those key moments in your decluttering process, like the initial sorting.

My ultimate goal when organizing the kitchen (and pretty much every area of the home) is to create a space that doesn't require removing multiple items to get to another. Of course, this doesn't apply to some areas—mainly in the kitchen—like nested mixing bowls or frying pans. I recognize that not all of us have unlimited storage space, multiple pantries, or huge kitchens, but I want you to avoid creating black holes filled with things unknown.

You want to create visibility to those deep cabinets and shelves so your belongings don't get lost or simply forgotten about. There is nothing better than being able to open a cabinet or pantry, know what you need, see it, grab it, and go.

## Sorting and Categorizing

My suggestion for sorting your kitchen is to work in the categories already there. Most homes, even those in serious disarray, still have most silverware, plates, and glasses organized together. Start with the utensils, sort, categorize and purge. Move on to the pots and pans. Repeat. Move on to the baking area. Repeat. Like in every space in your home, you want to have like-items, or similar categories, grouped together and MF'ers noted so that you can keep them at your fingertips.

> **Pro Tip:** have the smaller items in the front of a deep cabinet or closet so that if you do have to double up, you have visibility to what's in the back and, hopefully, not too much heavy lifting.

Personally, I am not a fan of certain kitchen gadgets and tools. While I know that some people absolutely love their garlic masher, vegetable chopper, or onion slicer, I find them completely overrated, totally a waste of space, and absolutely gratuitous. I know, I know, they are convenient and make uniform slices and dices, but in my opinion, all you really need is a good chef's knife and a knife skills class. You can even find tutorials on YouTube and save yourself the tuition. The 15 minutes of class and a little practice will give you the confidence to julienne like a pro and help you realize that a lot of these gadgets take up too much coveted space and are kind of unnecessary. And I know the professionals agree with me.

### Don't Take My Word For It

I consulted with Chef Ryan DePersio, Chef Partner of critically acclaimed New Jersey restaurants Battello, Fascino, and The Kitchen Step. His award-winning experience spans over 20 years and multiple continents and he appears regularly in the media, including segments on The Today Show and

The Food Network. So what does a professional chef of this magnitude consider to be his most important tools? His 10-inch Japanese Chef's knife and a diamond steel to keep it sharp. A necessity in any home chef's kitchen, DePersio says it "can be utilized in so many ways when it comes to cutting."

But I couldn't talk about one of my favorite areas of the home without also consulting one of my previous clients, Chef Tia M. D'Addario, Executive Chef and owner of Tia's Food and Love Catering Boutique in Verona, NJ. With over 32 years of experience, five of which she was awarded with the Best of Essex Awards for Best Caterer, I knew she wouldn't steer us wrong. She agrees, "there is just no substitute for having a set of really good knives in your kitchen. Besides being much safer, having sharp knives helps get through tasks with so much ease." In addition, she stresses the importance and versatility of one of her favorite appliances, the food processor, "I use it to make pie crust. I use it to make salad dressing. I use it to help me prep chopping vegetables. I use it to purée soups. I use it every time I cook, and it is invaluable."

Other tools that DePersio and D'Addario agree are **absolute staples** in any home kitchen:

- Microplane
- Serrated peeler
- Fish spatula
- Handheld potato masher
- Peeler
- Rubber spatula
- Kitchen mandolin
- Bottle opener

---

*"It's so hard, to say goodbye, to yesterday," – Boyz II Men*

---

But what about those items that should find their way to the recycle or donation bin? That's what I want to hear about. DePersio shared his list of top offenders:

- Corn holders - use your hands, it's more fun!
- Avocado slicer - just use a knife
- Flavor injector

- Pizza scissors - Never!
- Egg separator - get cracking!

D'Addario has similar opinions and great advice to get rid of any of the gadgets that have single-use purposes: "Usually these items can be replaced with something you already have."

- Strawberry huller - just use your paring knife
- Herb shears - a scissor works fine here
- Banana cutter - peel and eat! or use those trusty knives!
- Garlic press - a microplane grater or, you guessed it, use your knives!

## Letting Go

So in addition to the recommendations by our culinary experts, feel free to include the below items into your recycle bin or donation pile:

- Discard anything with chips, cracks, rust, or corrosion.
- Eliminate duplicates but be thoughtful with how many you truly need.
- Keep what serves the most purpose. Do you *really* need a cheese grater, a box grater, and a handheld rotary grater when they all essentially do the same thing? I got rid of my pop toaster when I got a toaster oven. No sense in keeping both.

> **Pro Tip:** if you do your dishes every night—which is really feasible if you have a dishwasher—you won't need more than one to two of each item.

- Edit down your coffee cup collection.
- Keep only what you use. Many of us fell into the bread making trend during the lockdown of 2020, but do you really need six bread tins?
- Eliminate Tupperware without lids or with stains.
- Get rid of all expired food and condiments.
- Donate unused appliances.
- Remove any unused cookbooks.

# Layout and Zones

Kitchens are also great places to start because the structured layout provides direction when deciding where to put something. A good approach is to arrange the contents of your cabinets and drawers based on:

1. The zones of your kitchen
2. What your cooking style is (this helps dictate your MF'ers)
3. The size of the items

The basic zones in a kitchen are:

- Food Prep
- Cooking
- Storage
- Clean-up

While these zones can help guide you on where to put certain items (as you'll benefit from having certain tools closest to these areas), don't feel limited to this approach. It's about creating a flow that is convenient and functional for you. You have to make your space work for you and your everyday routines, which include your cooking and eating habits.

> Do you cook a lot? What tools do you use most often? Are you a baker? Which supplies are you constantly searching for? Do you order out almost every night? Do you make one family meal, or are individuals preparing dinner at different times? Use these questions to determine your MF'ers and ensure they are getting the prime real estate.

> Small space - if you have a small kitchen or space with minimal counters, look to add a free-standing bakers rack or island that will offer more surface area and additional storage

Below, we will drill down into each zone, what is in them, and the best places to store them.

**Food Prep** - Usually your largest counter space.

**Prep tools:**

Measuring cups, mixing bowls, measuring spoons, cutting boards, and anything used to prepare the food.

- Store these items close to wherever your biggest counter space or surface area is that you use to prepare your food.
- Use drawer dividers[1] for measuring cups, vegetable peelers, and other tools.
- Nest bowls in deep drawers using deep drawer dividers[2] or in lower cabinets.
- Store cutting boards upright in a cabinet using a bakeware holder[3], using an over the door cutting board holder[4], or displayed on a countertop as functional decor.

**Small appliances:**

Hand mixer, immersion blender, mini food processor, et cetera.

- Store together in designated storage spaces, like a cabinet or pantry. You can use open top bins or simply store them on a shelf.

**Large appliances:**

Crockpots, stand mixer, Instant Pot, food processor, et cetera.

- If you use these items frequently, store at the top or bottom of the pantry. Or, if they are not used frequently, store them in an alternate storage area outside of the kitchen.

**Cooking** - This includes the stovetop, oven, and microwave areas.

**Cooking tools:**

Pots and pans, hand tools like spatulas, tongs, and wooden spoons.

- Store pots and pans in cabinets near the stove top, or if you have limited space, add a pot rack[5] to the wall.
- Nest similar items of varying size and keep similar material together, i.e., cast iron with cast iron, or non-stick vs. stainless steel.

- I love keeping pans or smaller pots in that awkward bottom corner cabinet (you know the one that usually has the double tiered lazy Susan?[6] - we discuss these later), but if you opt to keep something else here, use a bakeware holder to stand pans and skillets upright or store in another lower cabinet.
- Store hand tools like spatulas in drawers near the stove top using drawer dividers, or contain them in a topless container to the right or left of the stove (depending on which is your dominant hand).
- Stack pot lids vertically in a cabinet using an adjustable rack[7], nested together with each pot, or use a pot lid organizer[8] on the back of cabinet doors.

**Bakeware:**

Cookie sheets, tins, cooling racks, and casserole baking dishes.

- Store sheets and tins vertically. If you have narrow cabinets, this is a perfect spot for them. If not, try to keep them closer to the oven or your prep area. You can use an expandable cookware rack[9], or you can repurpose a dish or file rack.
- Baking dishes can be stored nested inside of each other in lower cabinets or deep drawers.

**Food:**

If you do not have a designated pantry, store your food in cabinets directly above or next to your work station. If you have a pantry, utilize that space before storing food in the cabinets. (See next chapter on Pantries for more tips and tricks.)

Storage - This includes the pantry or cabinets where your tableware, serving ware, supplies, or food is stored, and can even include the refrigerator.

**Everyday dishes, glassware, and utensils:**

- Grouping similar styles and shapes will streamline your pile of dishes, bowls, glasses, or flatware.
- Store these items close to the dishwasher or sink for easy transfer once they are clean and dry.

- Use drawer organizers[10] for everyday utensils, and if you are tight on space, use space saving solutions.[11]
- Maximize vertical space by using risers[12] or under-shelf baskets[13] for dishes, smaller plates and bowls.
- Store mugs in a cabinet close to where you prepare coffee. You can stack them using shelf risers or mug stackers. Organize the mugs using a mug tree if you have a coffee station.
- Be conscious of how handles on cups or mugs are facing.
- If you're tight on space, alternate wine glasses: right side up/upside down.

**Serving and entertaining:**

Platters, serving bowls, and trays.

- Store your everyday serving ware close to your everyday plates and bowls.
- Because platters and trays are often less frequently used, store them closer to the dining room, on higher shelves in a pantry, or in a cabinet not considered prime real estate. You can nest these items or use dividers or shelf risers to maximize the vertical space.

**Food wrap and Tupperware:**

- Keep all food wrap, aluminum foil, and plastic bags together.
- Use a food wrap organizer or drawer dividers in a shallow drawer to keep these items organized and streamlined.
- If drawer space is limited, adjust a shelf in a cabinet close to your workspace to about three inch width and store food wrap here; another option is to use a wall mount container(s)[14] on the inside of a cabinet or pantry.
- Store Tupperware items in a drawer or cabinet either close to your work space area or close to the refrigerator.
- Nest containers of the same shape and material and sort by size. Corral lids using a lid organizer, or contain the sets together with the lids on and use drawer dividers.

<u>Cleanup</u> – This includes the sink, drying area, under the sink, or wherever cleaning supplies are located.

**Towels, rags, sponges, and cleaning solutions:**

- Store these items under the sink using clear drawers[15] or open bins[16], or use wall mount containers inside the cabinet to optimize space.
- Keep cleaning solutions away from the refrigerator or food.
- Store everyday napkins in a napkin holder on your counter or table.

**Here are a few things we should keep out of our kitchen cabinets:**

**Seasonal/Infrequently Used Appliances or Cookware:**

Think Kitchen Aid, Ice Cream Maker, or Bread Tins. If you do not use them frequently, do not assign coveted shelf space to these items. Instead, store them in another area of the home, either a closet or basement, where you can access them when you periodically need them.

**Indoor/Outdoor Party Supplies:**

This includes trays, disposable plates and silverware, decorations, and the like. Whether you host often or not, keep the party supplies in another area of your home when space is limited. By storing these items in a clear bin out of the way, you can keep them clean, visible, and ready to use when the time calls for it.

**Open Food Containers:**

The best place to store food is a pantry, but if you store your food in your cabinets (not everyone has a designated pantry), the best way to do it is by using airtight containers. Transferring your food can maximize space, avoid spills, and (more importantly) keep the pests away.

**Cookbooks:**

If you must keep them on hand, edit your collection down to two or three books you use most often and put them in a location that is not front and center, like a top cabinet over the refrigerator.

**Manuals:**

I'm a huge advocate for eliminating these entirely. Everything can be found online. But if you need to keep them for peace of mind, do not keep them in the kitchen. Instead, store these items in a utility closet, basement, or attic in a weathertight container out of the way.

**Linens:**

Keep your linens organized in a designated closet and out of the kitchen. You can also store them in your dining room in a sideboard or buffet. You risk soiling them with food or liquids and monopolize space needed for cooking tools and supplies that are used more frequently.

**Paper or Plastic Bags:**

As we move away from vendor-provided bags when we are shopping, the tendency to save these desirables is astounding, and they usually end up shoved in a space they don't belong. Keep these items organized in another area, like the laundry room or even your car. You can also use a bag organizer under the sink[17] if you are limited with space outside the kitchen.

To sum up, kitchen cabinets and pantry shelves (more on that in the next chapter), especially those at eye level, are PRIME REAL ESTATE. These areas should be saved for your MF'ers. To waste them on things infrequently used that generally don't belong in a kitchen is a sin!

Don't be afraid to adjust the shelf heights in your cabinets or pantry. If you have bigger platters or tall champagne flutes, measure them and adjust your shelves, if possible, to accommodate specific categories.

*You want to keep your MF'ers stored in middle or lower cabinets.*

Since lower cabinets tend to be larger and deeper than upper cabinets, they lend themselves to some of the bigger and bulkier items in your kitchen. I like to store my heavier pots and cast irons down below, even though they may not necessarily be an MF'er. Think Le Creuset Dutch Ovens or cast-iron skillets. It's easier on the back and much easier to pick up than when it's on a higher shelf or cabinet.

*You want to keep less frequently used* *items stored on top shelves*, things like small appliances and larger (often taller) serving pieces. It's also smart to keep appliance accessories (blades, mixers, etc.) in higher cabinets or shelves, especially if you have small children.

## Corner Cabinets

So many families struggle with this one particular cabinet in their kitchen. They are actually called *blind base corner cabinets,* because we are reaching blindly into them to retrieve whatever we may have stored there. They are dark, deep, and inaccessible and always a point of frustration and confusion for my clients.

**Pro Tip:** A great way to maximize space is to install a roll-out drawer system[18] in larger or deep cabinets. These areas tend to become black holes where things just get pushed to the back, forgotten, and never seen again. Don't be intimidated! It's fairly simple to install these drawers; they offer visibility to the entire cabinet and make grabbing your items much easier. They come in various materials, colors, sizes, and prices, and are a great way to level up your kitchen storage.

There has been some evolution in organizing solutions over the past years for this sore spot, including the two-tiered lazy Susan and the next generation blind corner pull-out.[19] Both of these options definitely help maximize the deep space, but the classic version, unfortunately, leaves some dead or wasted space. I highly recommend, if your kitchen does not already have these solutions in place, to explore the option of installation.

But the question always goes back to what to store in this awkward space. I would advise sticking to this guidance on what to keep on top vs. bottom cabinets (less frequently used and smaller/lighter items on top, and heavier, more frequently used items on bottom).

I've had people store spices, oils, or pantry food on the bottom blind cabinets and heavy appliances or pots on the top. Personally, I advise against this. In fact, the opposite would be more acceptable.

My favorite use for the bottom blind cabinet is your everyday pots and pans— it's where I keep mine in my own kitchen. I've also worked on kitchens where we store heavier appliances in this area. As for the top, I'm a huge fan of storing cocktail and wine glasses in this section. But you could also store larger serving platters or bowls, or even spices and oils on a tiered lazy Susan. But you need to do what works for you and your family. As always, be sure to contain smaller categories, like appliance attachments, and measure measure measure.

## Countertops

I love a kitchen with clear countertops; it definitely creates a better working environment when trying to prepare meals. But I know that it's not always an option. If you need to, only keep items you access every day on your counters, but remember, if you are creative and optimize your space properly, you may find that you can have empty countertops with open space to work freely.

Common items stored on kitchen counters and their alternatives:

- Knife Blocks – Inside a drawer close to your work space using drawer knife holders. You can use a drawer insert[20] to contain and keep your knives (and your hands) protected.
- Toaster Ovens – In a deep low cabinet, using a pull-out drawer system.
- Coffee Machines - In a designated coffee bar cabinet, using a pull-out drawer system; stored either close to or also containing coffee mugs.
- Spices – Stored in drawers or upper cabinets using tiered lazy Susans or tiered shelf risers.[21]
- Stand Mixer – Stored in the pantry, secondary storage (hall closet/basement), or somewhere else in the home if not used frequently.

## Everything But the Kitchen Sink

I find underneath the kitchen sink tends to be a dark abyss in most kitchens, where things just get shoved in. I feel like people like to just put everything and anything that has to do with household cleaning below the sink, and in the end, they often don't have a clue what's down there. If you have the room to store them somewhere else, I suggest removing all cleaners meant for other areas of the home. Do not store laundry or bathroom cleaner under your sink. Keep this area for kitchen cleaners only. An exception is carpet or rug cleaner, since the living room is usually off the kitchen.

You'd be surprised at how impactful a few pull-out drawers[22] or clear bins can be, or how much they change the functionality and look of underneath the kitchen sink. The reason is because they maximize the space! I like to use stacking pull-out drawers[23] and deep open bins in almost every kitchen cabinet under the sink I work on. They both come in a variety of sizes so you can customize your space. The drawers come with dividers, so you can easily separate the contents into smaller categories.

A few things to note about under the kitchen sink:

- Be sure to use plastic or metal containers that can be easily cleaned or wiped down. Even your cleaning supplies need to be cleaned, so avoid using fabric or wood storage underneath a sink.
- When measuring, consider any pipes or garbage disposals that will limit some of the height and depth in your storage solutions.
- Get creative with storing your garbage bags—it's almost always best to take them out of the box to maximize your space. You can use a free standing paper towel holder, or mount a rod on the door to spool the garbage bags. You can repurpose a refrigerator wine bottle holder to nest the roll in. You could also use a plastic container with handle openings and a lid.[24] By feeding the end of the garbage bag through the handle opening and closing the lid, you create a dispenser that keeps the bags nice and neat and out of sight.

In my own home, I use pull-out drawers with dividers to contain my dishwasher pods, sponges, hand brushes, Mr. Clean Dry Erasers, and extra washcloths. I keep a lazy susan on top that holds my MF'ers: my Windex and disinfectant wipes. I use another two tiered roll out drawer that houses all the dish soap and surface cleaners, with a top rack that I nest my garbage bags in. All of my heavy-duty cleaners are contained in another narrow deep open bin. Everything has a home.

- Under the sink is another great spot for Command hooks or wall mounted containers. You can use the inside of the cabinet to hang rubber gloves or dishcloths, or to house extra stock of sponges or rags. Just make sure there is enough space to close the cabinet before you attach anything.
- When using lazy Susans under the sink, you want to make sure they are deep to keep bottles and supplies from falling over.

## Junk Drawers

The dreaded junk drawer. We all have one, maybe two. But cleaning it out is easier than you think. It's honestly such a quick fix with such a gratifying feeling. What we need to recognize is that this drawer is usually junk— that's why it's called that. For most, it's the purgatory before the garbage, a holder of those "what if I need these one day?" type of questions we ask ourselves. This random screw? The broken piece of a toy? The extra birthday candles in a special color? Let them go. Refer to the 20/20 rule we talked about in chapter two.

**Pro Tip:** Once your junk drawer is empty and cleaned, use a piece of wax paper to trace the size and shape of the drawer. Bring the paper, and your measurements, to the store where you will buy your drawer organizers and play a little Tetris to figure out what will fit without the guesswork.

When clearing this space out, take out everything in its entirety and sort the categories. Really consider if there is a reason you are holding onto these items. Be thoughtful and ask yourself if they will serve you better by being stored with similar items in another location in the house, like screwdrivers (belong with the tools in the garage) or those children's medicine syringes (belong with the children's medicine in the bathroom closet). This drawer should not be filled with actual junk, but with miscellaneous items that you frequently use in your kitchen (or wherever the drawer is).

My family has a "hair care" section in the junk drawer in our kitchen; I learned this hack from one of my best friends. We basically keep brushes, hair ties, and travel-size hair products because we're constantly doing hair in the morning over breakfast before school. It's unconventional, but it works for us.

You may not have a "hair care" drawer. It could be something completely different, like a homework drawer or a first aid drawer. The point is, do what works for you, but don't feel because it's unconventional (or maybe even uncouth) that it doesn't belong in your kitchen. Being organized is about making YOUR life easier, not following a blueprint from some book or magazine.

In this space, I tend to avoid using expandable pre-made drawers. Once you sort the contents and determine what will live in your drawer, you can measure the biggest item of each category and buy individual containers[25] that fit together like a puzzle so that it works for you.

## Command Centers

This is where you keep your keys, your mail, important reminders, and can be a catchall when you empty your pockets at the end of the day. It can be a charging station and the last minute grab-and-go area before you head out the door.

Make sure to address this area daily. You don't want to miss the permission slip or bill you were supposed to get out because it was buried under a pile of junk.

- Use key hooks or a small dish/catchall to keep keys in one spot.
- Contain incoming mail with a bin, basket, or file organizer. At the very least, go through this weekly to avoid paper overload.
- Add a charging station.
- Use a corkboard for reminders or a family calendar.

## Water Bottles

I am shocked when I come to a new home and there isn't some sort of obsession with water bottles. Because it rarely happens. So, if you are like so many people and have cabinets and drawers of water bottles stacked on top of each other, overflowing and falling over, then you are not alone.

Do yourself a favor. Edit them down. I know you have your favorites, and maybe there is a purpose for each, or a good explanation for having multiples, but no one needs more than three, and even that's a stretch. Get rid of the promotional ones while you're at it. You know, those freebies you got from the work trip?

Once you have edited your collection down, designate a space for them. That means *one* space. Try to avoid storing them in multiple locations, like so many love to do. Give them a home. Whether it's a top cabinet, a shelf, or a drawer, contain them. On a shelf, you can use water bottle holders.[26] These holders are great because they can be stacked and hold multiple bottles.Deep drawer bins[27] or drawer dividers work if you store them in a drawer. And you can get creative; I've even repurposed an old wine bottle holder for a client. Your goal is to have a tight collection in a space that will secure them from falling over.

## Oh Baby!!!

Babies come with so much stuff! Bottles, nipples, bottle cleaners, and formula bags… If you are blessed to have a little bundle of joy, congratulations! Now, do yourself a favor and designate an area just for baby. Assign a drawer and/or cabinet, out of baby's reach, that contains everything you need for feeding. This will make meal prep when you are sleep deprived and feel like a zombie just a bit easier.

Use drawer dividers[1] in deep drawers or clear storage bins[15] in a cabinet to corral bottles and contain all the baby feeding necessities. Then, as you move to solids, it will make for an easy transition to all of the children's dishware, water bottles, and lunch boxes that will soon take over.

## Children's Dishware

Do you share your cabinets or drawers with your children's plastic wear? Well, don't. Make a separate space for them. I always advise parents to keep a kid drawer easily accessible for little ones. It helps build confidence and a feeling of empowerment when they can get something for themselves or even help with the dishes. And it's one less thing for you to do, am I right? It will give them a sense of independence and give you back some cabinet real estate and a bit of sanity. Without any fancy risers or cabinet organizers, you can see the difference in your kitchen cabinet by simply removing all that BPA-free goodness.

- Designate a lower shelf or drawer for children' bottles, cups, and dishes so they can reach it. Corral their cutlery with a drawer organizer and store near the "adult" cutlery.
- Deep drawer dividers or deep bins help keep bottles and cups from falling over and makes it easier to maintain the order.

**Bonus Tip:**

- If your storage area has wire shelving, consider replacing it with wooden shelves, and for a more affordable option get shelf liners[28] to keep smaller items, contents, or bins from falling through the cracks or getting stuck. They come in a variety of lengths and widths.

 Take a picture! #igotdeecluttered

## Favorite Products:

- [1] Expandable Bamboo Utensil Tray, The Container Store
- [2] iDesign Linus Adjustable Deep Drawer Dividers, iDesign
- [3] mDesign Steel Storage Tray Organizer Rack, Amazon
- [4] Ashley Over the Cabinet Cutting Board Holder, Macy's
- [5] Old dutch wall mount bookshelf pot rack, Amazon
- [6] Rev-a-Shelf Lazy Susan, Amazon
- [7] Tower Adjustable Pot Lid and Frying Pan Organizer, William Sonoma
- [8] Evelots Pot Lid Storage, Wayfair
- [9] youCopia StoreMore Expandable Cookware Rack, The Container Store
- [10] Masirs Bamboo Kitchen Drawer Organizer, Amazon

- [11] Joseph Joseph DrawerStore Bamboo Compact Cutlery Organizer, Macy's
- [12] Tosca Dish Riser, The Yamazaki Home
- [13] Plate Undershelf Organizer, The Yamazaki Home
- [14] iDesign AFFIX Plastic Wall Mount Organizer, Amazon
- [15] The Home Edit Stackable Drawer, The Container Store
- [16] The Home Edit Stacking Pantry Bin, The Container Store
- [17] Simple Human Wall Mount Grocery Bag Holder, Amazon
- [18] Knape & Vogt Soft Close Wood Drawer Pull Out, Amazon
- [19] Rev-a-Shelf 2 Tier Organizer, The Home Depot
- [20] Rev-a-Shelf 2-Row Trimmable 55 Slot Knife Block, Amazon
- [21] 3-Tier Bamboo Expanding Spice Shelf, The Container Store
- [22] Double Drawer Wire Pull-Out Cabinet Organizer, The Container Store
- [23] The Home Edit Stackable Drawer, The Container Store
- [24] Nordic Basket with Bamboo Lid, The Container Store
- [25] Everything Organizer Drawer Organizer, The Container Store
- [26] mDesign Plastic Water Bottle Storage Organizer Rack, Target
- [27] IDESIGN Deep Drawer Bin, Target
- [28] Gorilla Grip Wire Shelf Liner, Amazon

# CHAPTER 5:

# Pantries and Food Storage

Whether you have limited space and store your food in your kitchen cabinets, or you are blessed with a walk-in pantry that is worthy of a feature in Better Homes & Gardens, we will go through some of the best ways to categorize and store your food supply.

## Letting Go

Discard any expired items. If an item has no expiration date and you don't remember buying it, get rid of it. Discard any opened products that have become stale or look questionable.

Relocate any items that are not food or food related.

## How to Store

If you find deciding what the best way to store the different categories of foods challenging, you are not alone. Use your gut and stick to what you and your family prefer. For example, my husband refuses to decant his Cheez-Its. **Decanting is transferring the contents of your item into another container.** He likes snacking on them from the box, and there was

**Pro Tip:** Don't forget that once you are done editing down and purging your pantry, do a grocery store run and stock all items you use consistently. You want to make sure that you are not missing any categories that you normally have on hand. Having a true representation of what you are planning to store is the point of this process, so having a fully stocked pantry or refrigerator is necessary to understand your inventory.

no changing his mind on that. He did, however, like the idea of an airtight cookie jar for his, I mean the children's, Oreo cookies. And sometimes, when I have time, I stack them like the Kardashians. Pick your battles and remember that it's not always necessary to decant your entire pantry out of the original packaging.

If you do decide to decant, I recommend using airtight food storage containers for dry goods stored in the pantry or cabinet. Square containers[1] are my favorite option because they stack perfectly and eliminate the dead space that rounded containers often create. Just be sure that you are ready and willing to maintain the process of decanting. If you're not up for filling and refilling and keeping track of expiration dates, then seriously give thought when deciding how many items you want to decant, which shape and sizes are best, and if this practice is really for you.

Very early on in my organizing journey, I hate to admit it, but I went out and spent about $500 on a ton of airtight food storage containers for every category of dry food staple in my pantry in every size imaginable. What a waste of money! You only need to decant the foods that *you use frequently* and that you're willing to actually maintain. For me, it's cereal (three different types), flour, sugar, pancake mix, breadcrumbs, granola, nuts, rice, spaghetti, and of course the cookies.

*"Like a moth to a flame, burned by the fire..."*
*— Janet Jackson*

But for the love of all that is holy, **get rid of the outer packaging**. This is especially true for your dried goods and if something is individually wrapped and then packaged again in outer packaging. Get rid of the outer boxes or plastic wrap—I'm not just talking about individual snack packs for your children's lunches, but all your dry goods, sponges, paper towels, or granola bars. Not only will it look less cluttered (plastic bags never look good) and save you room because all that packaging is truly a waste of space, but keeping all that cardboard can be the source of **<u>PANTRY MOTHS!</u>**

*"It's not about the pasta!" – DJ James Kennedy*

Decanting is not just about making a picture-perfect pantry to keep up with all the celebrity photos out there, there is a practical and preventative reason behind it. Not only does it keep your dry goods fresh and allow for easy access to goods you buy in bulk, but it also decreases the risk of those pesky pantry moths. Pantry moths are a real thing, and they don't just stick to the pantry. There have been many cases where moths infiltrate your home and your storage through dry food packaging or paper boxes, get comfortable, lay eggs, and result in a costly expense to get them removed. Consider yourself warned.

**Pro Tip:** When restocking a jar or container that is not completely empty with fresh contents, grab a bowl or smaller container, empty the old contents, and then fill the now empty jar with the fresh. Top off with the old contents, et' voila. First in first out. For expiration dates, use a label or even a piece of masking tape and write the date on the back of the container for a clean look.

If you are still anti-decanting, there are a number of options to storing your pantry staples that don't include this process, like using bag clips to keep cereal fresh and filing your multiple bags in a basket or clear rectangular storage bins designed for deeper pantry cabinets[2] which can hold all your boxes of food.

**Pro Tip:** A great way to keep track of the recipes that come on the back of your dry ingredients that you are decanting, like your pancake or cake mix, is to cut out those recipes and attach it right to the back of your airtight bin using some good old scotch tape.

## Layout, Zones, and How to Store

Remember, don't be afraid to adjust the shelf heights in your cabinets or pantry. Measure taller items like cereal boxes and make sure that you are storing them upright with the packaging labels facing out.

Make sure that you are storing your MF'ers on your middle shelves. Ready to eat food should also be at the middle shelf, usually at eye level. When you have little ones, if you're okay with them helping themselves, keep the healthy snacks at their eye level.

Food not stored at eye level tends to be eaten less frequently, so make sure that whatever you are storing on upper shelves is labeled clearly and positioned so that they don't disappear into the black hole, never to be seen again.

If you have a corner shelf in a pantry, a great way to maximize space is to use a lazy Susan. While these solutions cause some dead or wasted space, they are a great way to avoid forgetting things or losing them in the dark abyss of the back corner.

Overflow, backstock, and heavier products like drinks should be stored on the bottom or floor of the pantry, labeled, and corralled in a basket, bin, or crate.

For those items that cannot be decanted, like canned goods or specialty jars, it's best to display and arrange them in a way that allows visibility. This helps avoid having expired foods or overbuying. Below are some common ways to store these items:

- Oils and vinegars should be stored on lazy Susans.[3] Use one for each category depending on the number of different types you keep on hand.
- Canned goods should be stored on a stackable can rack organizer or a three-tiered expandable shelf.[4]
- For everyday items in pantries, like snacks, condiments, and ingredients you use to make dinner, it's important to use shorter containers[5] which make retrieving items easier, and containers that are clear or open to allow visibility. Try to keep categories in one bin or zone. Depending on your inventory, sometimes a zone can include multiple bins.
- Use taller bins[6] in pantries for backstock, or supplies used less frequently

Pantry categories are listed below. I've grouped them based on subcategories that will help guide you further if you are struggling on how to group your items. These subcategories can be grouped together on a shelf or combined in a bin if you are working with a smaller space or smaller amounts of food. I've also included some of my favorite solutions for certain subcategories. Feel free to use these or play around with what looks good, what fits, and what works for you.

| Categories for Food Stored in the Pantry | | | |
|---|---|---|---|
| **Category** | **How to Store** | Category | **How to Store** |
| **Breakfast** | Including oatmeal, pancake mix, etc. can be decanted using airtight bins or stored in a short bin for easy access | **Oils and Vinegars** | Store in a deep divided lazy Susan to keep items from falling over or in a deep bin depending on the size of the bottles |
| **Cereal** | Store using airtight cereal containers or by removing plastic bag from the box and securing with bag clips then file fold in bin, or file in original packaging | **Sauces** | Store on three-tiered shelves or in a short bin to allow visibility |
| **Bread** | Store in airtight bread container or keep in the plastic and store in a bin | **Spreads** | Store in a deep divided lazy Susan or short bin |
| **Coffee/Tea** | If individually packed, take out and store in an acrylic drawer or smaller container. For bulk, you can decant into airtight containers | **Condiments** | Store in a deep divided lazy Susan or short bin |
| **Sweeteners** | | | |
| **Snacks** | If individually packed, remove from outer packaging and file fold in a short or open bin. If kept in original packaging, store in open or clear bin for easy access | **Crackers** | Filed in a large bin |
| **Kids Snacks** | | **Nuts/Seeds** | Decant into an airtight container and store in an open bin |
| **Chips** | Use bag clips and file in a bin | **Dried Fruit** | Decant into an airtight container and store in an open bin |
| **Dips** | Keep in the same bin as chips or nearby in a small container | **Candy** | Decant and store in a candy jar |

| Category | How to Store | Category | How to Store |
|---|---|---|---|
| Dinner | Store in a shorter bin for visibility | Canned Goods | Categorize by type (fruit, vegetable, soup, sauce, etc.) and store on tiered shelves or can dispensers |
| Pasta | Decant into airtight containers or store in original boxes and place in labeled bins | | |
| Rice/Grains | | | |
| Beans | | | |
| Flour | Decant into airtight container | Baby | Contained in an open bin |
| Baking | Decant into airtight container in a separate bin | Pet Food / Supplies | Decant into decorative, airtight pet treat containers in a decorated pet basket |
| Drinks | Store in crates on the floor or out of plastic packaging on a shelf | Shakes / Supplements | Store in a deep basket or bin |
| Hot Chocolate | Mix to be decanted, individual packs to be taken out of cardboard packaging and stored in a small open bin | Vitamins | Store in tiered shelves or in a small open bin |

*"These pretzels are making me thirsty!" – George Kastanza*

## Snacks

Whether your family decants or leaves them in the original packaging, keeping your snacks at eye level helps avoid overbuying and is the best way to ensure that this frequently accessed category doesn't go bad or get forgotten about.

- Be thoughtful when you are stocking your pantry and don't buy more than you can store, meaning if you have limited space, refrain from getting your snack supply from places like Costco or Sam's Club. If possible, buy less more often, and do your best to designate a small space in your home (garage, basement, spare closet) for your backstock if necessary.

- If you have a door to your pantry, save shelf space for bigger items and opt to use an over the door organizer.[8] This beauty can be used to store snacks or other smaller item categories from your pantry. For a more affordable option use plastic shoe organizers for snacks and other non-opened items.

- You can get creative with how you store your variety of chips and other bagged foods. Use bag clips and file upright in a deep bin. You can also use an expandable vertical organizer[9] or repurpose a magazine rack to keep bags standing up and visible on a shelf.

- If storing snacks on a shelf or cabinet, you can use a divided lazy Susan.[10]

- If storing snacks in a deep drawer, be sure to use drawer dividers or deep containers. Both options help to contain subcategories and keep items from falling over. You can also use airtight or lidded containers to hold individual types or categories of snack items.

- Avoid using hidden storage systems[11] for frequently

**Mom Tip:** When organizing my children's lunch snacks (you know those beautifully packaged individual servings of childhood deliciousness?) I set it up once. I fill the open bin with about a week or two worth of each type of snack. I do my best to keep the same or similar sized foods together. I file them all in three to four columns. Everything is standing upright, like little soldiers at attention, but not stuffed to where things get completely squished. I put the remainder of my Costco supply in a back-up pantry and try not to worry about it again until the bin starts to become empty. I'm not constantly fixing and re-filling and making it look like a pinterest photo every day—ain't nobody got time for that! Set it once, refill when you are down to just a few options, and call it a day.

accessed food in a pantry. I like to reserve these (which are often sturdy fabric or linen) for non-food pantry staples like back up paper goods, candles, or storage wrap.

## Spices

There are so many options when it comes to storing your spices. The most popular option is in a drawer, followed by a cabinet, but the best space is within reach of your food prep area or stove for easy access. Just be sure wherever it is, it's a cool, dark, and dry space. Heat, light, and humidity will make your spices lose flavor more quickly.

### Letting Go of Spices

First things first: you need to clean out your spices. Now, I've been challenged a number of times by clients who are reluctant to get rid of their expired spices. I understand their sentiment, because spices don't really "go bad" the way milk or yogurt goes bad with the potential of making you sick. They just lose their freshness, potency and flavor over time, thankfully nothing that will actually make you spend your night praying to the porcelain Gods. But if your goal is using them to add some spice or zest to your meals, why waste space holding onto things that will result in bland, tasteless food?

So it's best to use your judgment: if your expired spices have a lackluster smell or no smell at all, it's time to say goodbye. Generally speaking, ground spices lose their flavor faster than whole spices, usually at about six months to a year past the expiry date. Whole spices last a lot longer and can last past the date by about four to five years.

If your spices have begun to clump, or have gone hard, it's probably safer to let them go. The potential of moisture is pretty high in this case, which means the chance of mold spores growing is also pretty high. When in doubt, throw it out.

---

*"Every boy, every girl!! Spice up your life!! People of the world!! Spice up your life!!" – Spice Girls*

---

While images and videos of people's beautifully manicured and decanted spice collections infiltrate my feed, I find the majority of people opt to keep their assortments in the original packaging. Remember, it's not necessary to decant your spices, you can still achieve a similar organized look by keeping them the way they came. There are plenty of options of how to store them once you decide where you will contain them. We will explore the two most popular below:

**Pro Tip:** If you decide to decant your spices: Use a funnel for easy transfer, label as you go to avoid confusion, and be sure to keep a few extra empty jars on hand for when recipes introduce new spices to your mix.

**Drawer or Cabinet?**

**The Spice Drawer:**

Who doesn't love the uniform look of beautifully decanted spices in a drawer using tiered acrylic spice risers?[12] Having them at an angle in a drawer gives you visibility to your entire collection and helps make it easier to grab them.

If you opt for this method, just be sure to measure your drawer height, width, and depth and buy the risers and jars that are compatible with the drawers and each other. You can run into challenges when you have bottles that don't fit. There are a number of expandable drawer organizer options out there to accommodate narrow or wide drawers.

**Pro Tip:** If you find there is a gap between your risers and your drawer, it even happens to professionals, you can use a drawer divider[13] (in the same material of the rack you're using) to fill the gap.

There is a controversial opinion out there that some of these slanted organizers actually take up more space than the jars alone. So, some alternative options are to use a spice drawer liner[14] or to lay square jars[15] flat to keep them from rolling out of place. If you have deep drawers, you can store your jars upright with the labels displayed on the top of the bottle.

**The Spice Cabinet:**

The spice cabinet offers more flexibility and can accommodate your range of jar sizes or vast collection of spices. It's also another reason why it makes using a cabinet a popular option when keeping your spices in the original packaging.

**Pro Tip:** When organizing your spices, keep MF'ers front and center. You can also alphabetize your collection for finding what you need quickly and easily, or if your culinary skills span a variety of countries and cultures you can opt to sort them by cuisine.

The following solutions can be used individually or in combination of each other to get the best use of your cabinet space. Just be sure to measure everything including the sizes of your largest containers you plan to store. You want to make sure everything is visible and not crammed in, this way you can avoid jars or packets falling into the black hole never to be seen again.

Some of my favorite cabinet solutions include:

- Cabinet mounted vertical spice drawer[16]
- Wall mounted spice rack[17]
- Single or tiered lazy Susans[18]
- Tiered spice or can risers[19]

# Refrigerator

Having your refrigerator organized is more important than you think, and I understand when people don't make it a priority. I didn't always have my refrigerator organized. To be honest, it was one of the last spaces in my home to be addressed. I don't know why that is, maybe because it seems just a little too extra, or maybe because investing time and money in an area of constant turnover made me hesitate to commit. But then I learned that not all shelves in your fridge are created equal. Game changer. Not only did updating the set up of my refrigerator save me time in the long run, like when I am trying to get the children fed and out the door or rushing to get dinner on the table, but it keeps my food fresher longer, and helps make overbuying a thing of the past.

Naturally, I always kept a certain, albeit small, level of organization to my fridge. But it was a little lacking. I kept ready to eat fruit and vegetables front and center, the meat on the bottom to avoid leaks or cross contamination, veggies in the crisper, and leftovers grouped where I could (hopefully) see them. But I also had condiments in the back, and milk in the door. Some refrigerators have a long thin drawer at the bottom. I always group my different cheeses and deli meats there. Wrong!

In case you're not aware, the door is the warmest spot in the fridge, and milk shouldn't go there. Thankfully, my children really don't let milk come close to spoiling in our fridge. But still, the door is where condiments (like salad dressing, butter, margarine, jams, mustards, salsas, pickles), juices, soda, wine and things with preservatives should be stored since they can withstand the lower and sometimes fluctuating temperature of the door.

The top shelf is the next warmest spot in the fridge. This is where leftovers, soon to expire items, or things that need to be reheated should go.

As you go down the shelves, it gets colder. So naturally things like yogurt, milk, sour cream, cottage cheese, and eggs should go next on the middle shelf or shelves.

When it comes to fruits and vegetables, I always kept them in the crisper but stored my apples separately because I knew that the ethylene gas they emitted caused the other fruits to ripen faster. What I didn't know is that there are other foods that belong in the same family. These foods emit this gas and should all be stored in a drawer with a low humidity setting to keep fresh and from spoiling others. See below for the two groups of fruits and veggies that should be kept separate:

| Refrigerator Drawer Storage Categories | | |
|---|---|---|
| **Low Humidity Setting - open window** | | |
| high ethylene gas producers | | |
| Apples | Kiwi | Apricots |
| Avocadoes | Mangoes | Cherries |
| Cantaloupes | Papayas | Nectarines |
| Figs | Pears | Peaches |
| Honeydew | Plantains | Plums |
| **High Humidity Setting - closed window** | | |
| sensitive to moisture loss, and tend to wilt | | |
| Arugula | Cucumbers | Peppers |
| Asparagus | Eggplant | Raspberries |
| Broccoli | Green Beans | Squash |
| CauliFlower | Greens | Strawberries |
| Citrus | Lettuce | Sweet Potatoes |

Lastly, you should keep meat and fish at the bottom. Not only is it the coldest spot, but you avoid the chance of raw meat dripping on the rest of your food.

I love to use additional drawers[20] to separate grab-and-go fruits and vegetables from pre-packed lunch snacks, and veggies to be cooked from specialty jars or bottles. Personally, I find that the containers with lids create an extra step and a need to remove one thing to get to another, but do what works for you and your family. Just remember to measure every inch if you are going to go out and buy refrigerator storage. Try to utilize all vertical space. You can double stack deep drawers on a tall shelf or adjust the shelves to hold a row of uniform drawers or bins.

Regardless of your refrigerator setup, don't be afraid to play around with the shelf heights to create what works for you. As long as you consider the temperature of each area and group categories where they would benefit with extended shelf life, you'll save money and avoid food waste.

Experts agree that you should aim to keep the temperature of your fridge between 34 and 39 degrees Fahrenheit. Items you don't need to keep in your fridge include:

- Bananas
- Potatoes
- Tomatoes, unless they are ripened and beginning to soften
- Onions
- Pumpkin
- Winter Squash (acorn, butternut, and spaghetti)

**Pro Tip:** Don't forget to leave enough room for your tallest bottle or container. Measure the height and make sure you have enough space for it when configuring your shelves. Be sure not to store the larger or taller items in a position where they are blocking the vents and trapping the air. And remember to leave space on the middle shelf for the milk!

Here is a quick guide to what belongs where in a refrigerator:

| Refrigerator Location Guide | | | |
|---|---|---|---|
| Refrigerator Location | Temperature | What to Store | Examples |
| Door | warmest, most fluctuating | condiments and drinks | salad dressing, butter, margarine, jams, mustards, salsas, pickles, juices, soda, wine |
| Top Shelf | next warmest after the door, back of top shelf being the coldest | leftovers, pre-cooked foods, deli meats | foods to be reheated, or about to expire |
| Middle Shelf | next coldest after the top shelf | dairy, dairy based drinks | cheese, yogurt, milk, sour cream, cottage cheese, and eggs |
| Bottom Shelf | coldest temperature | meat/fish | |
| Crisper Drawers | low and high humidity (see refrigerator door storage chart) | vegetables | (see refrigerator door storage chart) |

And here is just a friendly reminder that you shouldn't believe that you need to spend a lot of money to get a functional setup in your own kitchen. It is totally possible to do it affordably. You can go to Home Goods or Big Lots and find inexpensive acrylic drawers, lazy Susans, or open bins.

### Freezers

Make sure you measure your freezer to ensure that you are making the best use of all the available space and purchasing the best-fitting storage bins.

Create zones in your freezer by food type, for example frozen vegetables, meats, breakfast foods, desserts, ice packs, and frozen dinners. It's best to use freezer safe storage bins[21] to store items vertically instead of laying them flat to maximize the space. By having visibility of your food and using labels on storage bins, you reduce the risk of wasting food and money.

Be sure to do a periodic inventory of your frozen foods. Food kept in the freezer past a certain point will not make you sick, but it will definitely lose texture and flavor. According to the United States Department of Agriculture, the suggested storage times for keeping frozen food varies and are listed below:

**Pro Tip:** When you're storing food that is room temperature in the freezer, position the bag so that it lies flat until it is completely frozen through. Do this for things like ground meat, sauce, or soup. Once it is frozen, you can file it in one of your designated bins and save yourself some space!

| Frozen Food Shelf-Life Guide | |
| --- | --- |
| **Item** | **Months** |
| Bacon and Sausage | 1 to 2 |
| Casseroles | 2 to 3 |
| Egg Whites or Egg Substitutes | 12 |
| Frozen Dinners and Entrees | 3 to 4 |
| Gravy, Meat, or Poultry | 2 to 3 |
| Ham, Hotdogs, and Lunch Meats | 1 to 2 |
| Meat, uncooked Roasts | 4 to 12 |
| Meat, uncooked Steaks or Chops | 4 to 12 |
| Meat, uncooked ground | 3 to 4 |
| Meat, cooked | 2 to 3 |
| Poultry, uncooked whole | 12 |
| Poultry, uncooked parts | 9 |
| Poultry, uncooked giblets | 3 to 4 |
| Poultry, cooked | 4 |
| Soups and Stews | 2 to 3 |
| Wild Game, uncooked | 8 to 12 |

Storing leftover pizza: Now, one of my best friends doesn't save leftover pizza. I know there must be people out there who are like her. So, for all of you who are turned off by leftovers, including my best friend, feel free to skip this section. But for the rest of us, let me share my secret. I am an over-orderer by nature. My problem stems from several factors: I love food and I eat a lot of it. I also have plate envy, meaning if you order something that I didn't order, I usually want what you have in addition to my own food—sometimes in place of. I also would rather have a taste of five different dishes, or at least bites of those five different dishes, than one dish in its entirety. And lastly, my eyes are bigger than my appetite, to some extent. So, when I order food, there are usually leftovers. Especially pizza. And instead of just wrapping the leftover pizza with tinfoil and throwing it in my freezer, I get out my Sharpie. I label the pizza. I label the date, the pizzeria, and what type of pie it is. My children only eat plain slices, and we are all partial to Forte's Ristorante and Pizzeria in Caldwell, NJ. So instead of opening multiple slices to find what I'm looking for, having everything labeled makes pizza selection on leftover night a lot easier. It also helps me know how old the slice is. So obviously, we use the first-in first-out rule, and if it's a *really* old slice of pizza, then it finds its way to the garbage disposal.

**Bonus Tips:**

- Taking the extra time to properly rinse and store your produce and storing them in a location best suited based on temperature helps extend the shelf life.
- If your pantry has wire shelving, like I mentioned in the kitchen, consider replacing it with a wooden shelf. For a more affordable option: get shelf liners to keep smaller items from falling through the cracks or getting stuck. They come in a variety of lengths and widths and are available on Amazon.
- Unless you are lucky enough to have a second refrigerator in your home or garage, make sure to leave some empty space on a shelf for an unexpected purchase or gift.

**Favorite Products:**

- [1] OXO POP Food Storage Container, Walmart
- [2] IDESIGN Deep Drawer Bin, Target
- [3] mDesign Modern Metal Lazy Susan Turntable Basket Tray, Target
- [4] Lenwi Spice Rack Organizer for Cabinet, 3 Tier Expandable Bamboo Spice Storage, Amazon
- [5] Urban Stackable Wire Basket in Medium or Large, The Container Store
- [6] Urban Stackable Wire Basket in Deep, The Container Store
- [7] OXO POP 4.5qt Airtight Large Cereal Dispenser, Target
- [8] Elfa Utility Large Wire Over The Door Rack, The Container Store
- [9] YouCopia StoreMore Expandable Cookware Rack, The Container Store
- [10] mDesign Lazy Susan Turntable Divided Spinner, Walmart
- [11] Large Kiva Storage Bins, The Container Store
- [12] Dingelex Expandable 4 Tier Acrylic Spice Rack Tray Drawer Organizer, Amazon
- [13] Qearl Drawer Dividers Organizers Adjustable 3.2" High, Amazon
- [14] YouCopia SpiceLiner Spice Rack Drawer Organizer, Amazon
- [15] Netany 24 PCs Spice Jars with Labels, Amazon
- [16] Vertical Spice 4-Shelf Cream Cabinet Mount Spice Rack, The Home Depot
- [17] Double Acrylic Spice Rack, The Container Store
- [18] SimpleHouseware 2 Tier Turntable Lazy Susan Spice Organizer, Amazon
- [19] Everything Organizer Large 3-Tier Organizer With Drawer, The Container Store
- [20] The Home Edit Divided Fridge Drawer, The Container Store
- [21] YouCopia FreezeUp Freezer Bin, Amazon

# CHAPTER 6:

## *Master Bedroom*

---

*"Your room is an externalization of your mind...*
*straighten up what you can straighten up."*
*– Jordan Peterson*

---

Organizing your closet is the best way to create a more relaxing space where you start and end your day. When you feel like you have nothing to wear, it's usually because you can't see what you have.

There are a number of factors that will affect how you organize your closet and dressers. For example, the size of your closet, whether you have more hanging space versus drawer space, the size of your wardrobe, and your lifestyle or MF'ers.

Your first step is to edit your wardrobe to only the best-fitted, most flattering clothes that make you feel confident and comfortable. Your closet should look like your own boutique. **When your clothes are not crammed into drawers or on racks, shopping your closet is much easier and more fun.**

## Letting Go

---

*"I'm Chandler, could I be wearin' anymore clothes?"*
*– Joey Tribbiani*

---

The dreaded closet purge. Deciding whether to keep something or let it go is hard for so many reasons. Here are a few items that you should not hesitate to let go of:

- Damaged clothing (garments with holes that are ripped, torn, or stained beyond repair)
- Clothes that were gifts, but just not your style or fit (it's okay to let go, I promise)
- Promotional T-shirts (free giveaways)
- Bridesmaid dresses
- Purses that are damaged, or that you will not use anymore
- Uncomfortable or broken shoes
- Socks with holes or that are missing a pair
- Belts that are damaged or do not fit
- Scratched or damaged sunglasses
- Broken jewelry or earrings missing a pair
- Hats that do not fit
- Anything borrowed (get it back to the rightful owner)
- Expensive mistakes—anything that you're afraid to let go of because it was a costly mis-purchase

## Prime Time

So many of us hold onto items that are past their prime, because we are hoping that we'll fit into them one day or because they spoke to us in the past. But ask yourself this: is an outfit representative of who you are today and your current style? Or the person you were 10-15 years ago?

> I had a client who held on to these Adidas tracksuits he bought in the 90s because it was one of his first big stylish purchases, and they meant so much to him. He even bought them in two colors. He wore them all the time, and he still had them almost 30 years later. But the truth was, he couldn't remember the last time he wore them and recognized that he was holding onto them for nostalgic purposes. We even discussed the potential of passing them on to

his children or nephews, but unless items are truly designer pieces in good condition, the likelihood that anyone is going to want 40-year-old used clothing is pretty slim. But most importantly, he recognized that his style had evolved, and he was not the same person who once wore Adidas tracksuits. He knew it was time to let go of them.

## The COVID Effect

The COVID pandemic has changed the way most of us live and work, and not surprisingly, what our daily or work wardrobe looks like. And for many people, weight gain from those months and years locked in our homes is a real thing. Forget the "Freshman 15," I guess now we can call it the "COVID 19."

All this change has been a source of confusion and hesitation for people when deciding to keep or let go of excess clothes in their closets. Those tried-and-true guidelines of years past don't necessarily apply anymore. "Have you worn it in two years?" "Well, no, but the past two years my social life was abysmal," or "My weight has changed," or "Sweatpants are my new business casual."

## When Something Doesn't Fit

For those of you with fluctuating weight, or those on a weight loss journey, consider donating those clothes that are too small, and that you have been holding onto in the hopes of fitting into them one day. Most likely, they will be out of style, so why waste the coveted closet space on them? And what better way to reward your hard work and the new you than with some new clothes that flatter and fit your transformed body?

Maternity clothes and clothes you had during your weight loss journey (whether postpartum or not) can definitely take up coveted space in your closet. For maternity clothes: if you are not currently wearing these items, and planning on having more children, then store them in a clear bin with a lid and a label. If you are currently wearing your maternity clothes, designate a drawer or drawers for these clothes and swap them out for your everyday clothes that don't fit at the moment. Keeping them stored and organized will make that transition back so much easier, especially with your hands filled taking care of your new little one.

## To Keep or Not To Keep

As you go through all the items in your wardrobe, and each category of clothing, sort into those four groups: Keep, Donate, Recycle, and Relocate. Unless you are moving seasonal clothes to another location, or jackets to a spare closet, the "relocate" pile tends to be minimal.

The following questions are great to keep in mind when purging your closet:

- Do you love it?
- Do you wear it?
- Would you buy it again?
- Is it in good condition?
- Does it fit?
- Are you really going to repair it or get it altered?
- Does it project the image you want to portray?

If you answered no to any of these questions, it's probably time to say goodbye. You can repurpose damaged T-shirts or cotton fabric garments into rags, or research local companies that offer textile recycling services.

Once you have your piles to donate, recycle, and relocate, get those bagged up and out of the room. When you decide to part ways with any article of clothing, be confident in your decision and don't go rummaging back through the bag. Take comfort in the fact that, if you're donating it, someone who truly needs it will appreciate and benefit from your generosity. I find that people get such a sense of relief from editing down their wardrobes into quality pieces that they love and are actually excited to wear.

## Back to Basics

Everyone has those items they keep buying over and over. For some, it's black leggings, or like me, it's plain white tees. Whatever your shopping vice is, keep in mind that you don't need more than a week's worth of any article of clothing. Keep your favorites and those in the best condition and let go of the rest.

Why waste precious space on clothes you're not going to wear? And not just space, think of the time: the time you will waste searching, washing, and putting them away.

---

*"But tonight, I'm cleaning out my closet" – Eminem*

---

For all things fashion related, I turned to fashion industry veteran, Danielle Licata. I asked for her thoughts on the best way to avoid crowding your closet while keeping your wardrobe fresh and functional. Licata is the co-owner of Miami's hottest luxury destination for retail therapy: Curio at Faena Bazaar—a three story, 20,000 square foot boutique featured in Forbes, WWD, and Vogue magazines, to name a few. She has served as Vice President to Stella McCartney, North America, the Vice President, and General Manager of Coterie, and is a very dear friend.

> "They say that we wear 20 percent of our clothes 80 percent of the time. To get more use out of your clothes, start looking at your closet and your purchases strategically. First, identify the functional clothes in your closet that fit and are in good shape," these are what Licata calls your winners, items you wear often that make you feel comfortable. The rest—if it doesn't fit, is outdated, or is maybe only wearable one or two more times in your life for a special occasion—she says, "should all leave the closet, be given away, sold, or stored for a future dressy event."

Licata recommends making sure that you aren't just repeating buying more of what you already own when you shop. She advises replenishing and reviving "with a few items each season that are trend right—new patterns, colors, or silhouettes—which allow you to look relevant and feel good when you step out to work, dinner, events or parties." She educates her clients on new trends and encourages them to make sure they are refreshing and refining their look. "This is the real reason to buy new things," she says.

A great way to start your closet refresh is to update your basics (think first layer or underpinnings, like T-shirts or tank tops). Edit out the ones that are stained, stretched out, or pilled beyond repair. Investing in quality basics that you know you will wear every day helps save space and valuable time when deciding what to wear in the morning.

Every few years, I replace my basics. Whether it's camisoles, white T-shirts, or even underwear. When I was in my 20s, I kept stacks of white T-shirts, mostly with stains, stretched out camis, and socks with holes. That is really no way to live, and no way to keep a closet—it honestly adds time to getting ready in the morning.

Think about the difference between opening your T-shirt drawer, and unfolding not one or two, but three white T-shirts with no success, having to put them all back because one had stains, one had a hole, and one was turning yellow. Now your drawer is a mess, you have to stress about folding everything back, and you're still searching for a clean white shirt that you could have sworn was in there. Maybe it's in the laundry? Ugh, and now you're late, what a time suck! Now consider going into the same drawer and knowing that all your white shirts are in great condition. You pick up one of the beautifully folded shirts and put it on. You know which one it is because it is folded in a way that you see the tag and neckline. Your drawer is still organized, you are dressed, and you can move along with your day. Which scenario would you prefer?

Now I get it, some people are thinking, "Girl, are you crazy? I can't replace all my basics every few years. I don't have the money for that!" But you can update your closet inexpensively without going out and buying $80 T-shirts. There are quality options out there for every budget. Trust me. It's so important to edit your wardrobe down to the most functional and best fitting items, making sure you have the essentials, and caring for your clothes properly.

Licata recommends the following list of essentials for every women's wardrobe:

- Bodysuit or fitted underpinning (for under items such as blazers and jackets)
- 4-5 elevated basic T-shirts
- 2-3 white and black blouses
- 2-3 poplin tops
- Relaxed blazer
- Denim shorts and dress shorts
- Relaxed Jeans/Skinny Jeans
- Relaxed casual pants: jogger or cargo
- Leather leggings
- Wide leg trouser
- Perfect black skinny pants

For men, Licata recommends the following essentials:

- 3 - 4 Elevated Polo shirts
- 4 - 5 Pocket T-shirts in several colors (always freshen your T shirt selection)
- 5 - 6 Linen or cotton button downs in a variety of colors
- 2-3 Professional sweaters
- Lightweight versatile jacket (i.e., a bomber)
- 2 Item blazers
- 3 Colors of your favorite jean fit
- Relaxed but elevated travel or weekend outfit (in a sweat or tech fabric)
- White dress sneakers
- Suede dress sneakers
- A Killer fitted suit

# Hangers

If you haven't done this already, it's time to get rid of all the wire dry-cleaning hangers and all the plastic hangers that came free with a purchase. You will be surprised by the impact of eliminating all the dry cleaner's plastic and random hangers in a closet. It feels like a before and after makeover with just this step alone!

I prefer the no-slip space-saving velvet hangers[1] for most clothing categories, heavy-duty space-saving plastic hangers[2] for bulkier items like blazers or thin coats, and wood hangers[3] for most outerwear. There is a lot of movement away from the black velvet hangers because there are other options that don't cause pilling, or rub off on your clothes, but I still love using these. You can also opt for a lighter color of beige or grey for a fresh look. But regardless of which you choose, investing in uniform hangers is an instant upgrade, and elevates your closet in one step. While I require that my clients get rid of all wire hangers, I support saving those white plastic hangers or sturdy plastic hangers with clips. These are great for the laundry room or spare coat closet— but I do try to keep whatever clients hold onto uniform if possible.

## Layout and Zones

Like the other areas of your home, you need to consider how you currently use the space. How do you get dressed in the morning? Generally, we start by putting our undergarments on, then day clothes. At the end of the day, we put on pajamas before bed. But do you wear a suit every day? Or do you get up and go to the gym, so your first outfit of the day is exercise clothes?

The point is, when you consider your layout, you want to group the categories that you use together. No sense in walking back and forth across the room or closet when you're trying to get out the door. Use prime real estate for your MF'ers. Don't keep gowns and suits front and center if you wear jeans every day. Maybe you want to keep your socks next to your bed, or where you have a seat so you can immediately slip them on.

The goal is to create zones that make getting dressed and out for the day easy for yourself. The amount of clothing and accessories that you own will determine how specific you can drill down in each category.

General categories for drawers or shelves for both men and women are:

| Categories for Clothing Stored in Drawers | |
|---|---|
| Category | Subcategories |
| Undergarments (bras, bralettes, underwear, undershirts, shapewear, socks, tights) | Everyday bras/sports bras, lingerie, men's undershirts tank or tees, dress socks/athletic socks |
| First layer clothes (women's undershirts, camisoles, T-shirts, long sleeves) | Graphic tees, plain tees, elasticized or cotton camisoles |
| Mid layer clothes (sweaters, sweatshirts, turtlenecks) | Casual/dressy, graphic/plain, or drill down by fabric type |
| Bottoms (jeans, sweatpants, leggings, shorts) | Length: capri/full leg, cut, or fabric |
| Pajamas (sets, single pieces, negligée) | Fabric or season, print or solids |
| Loungewear (sweatpants, sweatshirts) | Fabric or season, print or solids, length of top or bottom |
| Exercise clothes (sports bras, tank tops, T-shirts, shorts, pants, mid layer, long sleeve, sweatshirts) | Sleeve or pant length, print or solids |
| Bathing suits | One piece or two piece for women, and trunk length for men |
| Coverups | Fabric and length for cover ups |

# Know When to Fold Em'

No matter what size of closet I encounter, there is always "never enough room." So, whether you have a tiny apartment with minimal closet space, a walk-in closet with an island, or even a beautiful custom closet with a showcase room for bags and shoes, folding your clothes efficiently creates more space and helps make putting your clothes away that much easier.

## Folding Clothes 101

I stand by the file fold. I do use the pile fold on my shelves with some of my bigger and bulkier sweaters, or my jeans that I keep folded in my closet. But for all drawers, it's file fold or bust. God bless whoever came up with file folding. Marie Kondo has coined the KonMari Method of folding, which is a perfect file fold. While I'm not sure if there were any other organizing pioneers before her, I am positive that she has been a major influence on the popularity of this technique.

Regardless, it really works in practically every drawer you're trying to organize. Whether you use dividers or not, bins or baskets, labels or no labels, it seriously is life-changing. Not only does it save a remarkable amount of space (I'm talking over half a drawer of recovered space), but it also gives visibility to what you have and decreases the probability of creating a mess! Three of my favorite things when getting decluttered.

The file fold is simple and can apply to any clothing category. With a simple search on the internet of "file fold" you will find several tutorials on how to master this technique. Basically, you want to create a rectangle with whatever you are folding, and fold from the bottom up into thirds (depending on the size of the garment, sometimes I make it a fourfold).

> If it's a tank top, lay the item flat, fold the two sides in, and the straps down to create that rectangle. Fold from the bottom up into thirds.

> If they are jeans or shorts, fold the item in half with the crotch facing inward. Tucking the crotch in a little more creates a nice rectangle, and now you can fold from the bottom up into thirds.

Speaking of crotch: underwear. Thongs, briefs, boxer briefs, I do it all the same way:

First, lay it flat. You want to create a "V" shape, then a small rectangle.

> With boxer briefs, fold in at the legs—the outer corner of the leg to the middle of the waistband to create a V. Fold the crotch up to the waistband, and then fold the left end of the waistband in, followed by the right. File with all folds facing the same way on its side.

> With thongs or briefs, you already have a "V" shape. So, you will only fold the crotch up to the waistband, then each side of the waistband in.

Regardless of what you are folding: tees, long sleeves, underwear, you want to fold each category in the same bin or drawer into *the same size*. This will ensure you maximize the space and visibility of each item, plus it looks nice. Consider this, you generally don't store legal-size folders with letter-sized folders, do you? The same goes for clothes.

Once you get the hang of it, it saves time putting away laundry, finding what you need when getting dressed, or packing for a trip, and it just looks great. You legit just pull forward from the back and file the clean clothes into the back of the drawer. This also helps rotate your clothes and keeps you from wearing the same things over and over.

**Pro Tip:** When folding my laundry, I usually keep one category item out as a guide. This way, I'm making sure that all of my tank tops, for example, are being folded the same size and will fit nicely into my drawer without having to refold anything.

Now, I wish that I could say that once you set up your drawers or shelves, they will stay neatly folded and beautiful for all eternity, but I can't. Sometimes it gets a little messed up, but with this system, it takes minutes to get back to that organized place.

A few tips for items folded in dressers:

- Keep undergarments and first layer pieces together as a zone where you get dressed in the morning (ideally in separate drawers).
  - Bras
  - Underwear
  - Socks
  - Camisoles or undershirts
- If your dressers offer thinner top drawers, opt to use these for smaller items, like underwear, socks, or even jewelry.
- Protect your sweaters with some sort of moth repellent, like cedar blocks[4] or sachets.
- Use drawer dividers[5] to keep your rows in order and categories separated, but you can elevate the look by using decorative fabric boxes or bamboo dividers.[6-7]

A few tips for pile folding:

- Fold categories the same size, whether you are using a traditional pile fold or the file fold.
- When you are storing clothes using the pile fold on a shelf, whether it's sweaters, jeans, or pants, use shelf dividers.[8] You can use ones that slide onto the shelf itself, or if you are working with thicker shelves or a bottom shelf, you can use modular shelf dividers with adhesive that attach to the shelf surface.

A few tips for file folding:

- If you have a shallow drawer, make sure the height of your fold is not taller than your drawer.
- If you want to file fold an item but are lacking drawer space, you can always use a bin, basket, or box on a shelf.
- If you are folding a graphic tee, fold the two sides in and ensure that the graphics are visible at the top of the second fold. This way, when you file them in your drawer, you actually know which tee it is.
- When your drawer or shelves start to get a little messy, take five minutes to refold the pieces (or the entire drawer or shelf if needed).

## Hangin' Tough

General categories for hanging both men's and women's clothing are listed below (depending on how you like to organize your closet, you can include any and all of the general categories for drawers or shelves in your hanging section):

**Pro Tip:** Follow the 5-minute rule: if it takes five minutes or less, then do it now. Clutter feeds on clutter. If you don't address the little clutter while it's little it will grow into even bigger, more unmanageable clutter.

| Categories for Clothing Stored on Hangers | | |
|---|---|---|
| **Category** | **Subcategories** | **Drill Down to Specifics** |
| Outerwear | Jackets | These can all be drilled down by fabric or style, solid or print, as well as length of sleeve or garment, and/or season |
| Outerwear | Blazers | |
| Outerwear | Vests | |
| Tops | Blouses | |
| Tops | Button Down Shirts | |
| Tops | Lightweight Sweatshirts | |
| Bottoms | Pants | |
| Bottoms | Skirts | |
| Bottoms | Dress Shorts | |
| Hanging | Gowns | |
| Hanging | Short Dresses | |
| Hanging | Rompers | |
| Hanging | Jumpsuits | |
| Hanging | Beach Cover-ups | |

*"Oh oh oh oh oh, Hangin Tough"*
*– New Kids on the Block*

A few tips for hanging clothes in a closet:

- People differ in their preference for how they arrange their hanging garments. Do you sort by type or by color? I personally like by type, and then color. It's easy on the eyes, and helpful when you are looking for a specific item. However you choose to arrange your hanging clothes, do your best to factor your MF'ers into deciding what gets prime real estate.
- If you have more than one category on a rod, use rod dividers[10] to create separation between categories and make it easier to find what you're looking for.
- Be mindful of the fabric. You will extend the life of your clothing if you care for it properly.
    - Don't hang heavy sweaters, as the weight will ruin the shape of the garment over time.
    - Be careful when hanging sequins or beaded garments next to softer wool or cashmere, as you risk snags and pulls of the fabric.
    - Do not fold silk. Place it gently on a hanger.
    - Never put a hanger through the neck of a garment. You can stretch out the top beyond repair. Always put the clothes on hangers by placing the hanger through the bottom of the garment.
- When hanging clothes, make sure you are hanging the garments in the same direction, and make sure that direction is facing where you stand when looking through the rack. Don't be afraid to face certain sections of your closet in different directions. If the layout calls for you to stand facing one direction when in front of one rod, versus another direction in front of another rod, adjust accordingly. This helps you see what you have, and the consistency of the garment's direction looks great.
- Avoid hanging long dresses or garments where they pool on the floor. This can cause wrinkles and you risk getting them dirty or dusty. Look into raising your rod, or if that is not possible, fold the garment over the hanger so it does not hit the floor.

- Store infrequently used hanging garments (like out of season clothes, or formal wear like tuxedos or gowns) in a separate space or in the closet's back or upper shelves.
- And remember, don't forget to maximize your space by using every inch—even previous dead zones like behind the door or the back corners of a closet.

## Accessories and Misc.

*"The only thing that separates us from the animals is our ability to accessorize." – Clairee Belcher*

Certain categories (generally smaller items or things you have smaller amounts of) lend themselves to being stored in streamlined structured bins, things like bathing suits, seasonal accessories, etc. However, a lot of accessory categories have specific organizers made just for them.

**Bags/Purses:**

If you have the room, showcase your bags! While some people prefer to store them in their dust bags, I think it's best to put them on display so you can see them. Out of sight, out of mind, right?

There are multiple options on how to store and display. Some of my favorites by type include:

- Clutches/evening bags: file them upright using clutch dividers.[11]
- Shoulder bags: hang using acrylic bag stands[12] You can also use a drop front sweater box[13] to offer more protection for your purses. By standing the box on its side to have the front swing open like a door, you create a perfect little cubby for your bags.
- Totes: use acrylic purse hangers[14] to hang them from a rod.

Whichever way you store them, use purse shapers[15] to help keep the form and make them stand upright. You can buy these specific products, or simply use dust bags, heavy duty tissue, or even bubble wrap.

## Shoes:

Whether you store your shoes in your bedroom closet or a mudroom, visibility makes getting ready much easier. While some people like to store shoes on angled, free-standing shoe racks[16], they don't always stay put. Others store using clear shoe boxes[17], but the time it takes to open and close, take out and put back defeats the purpose of getting dressed with ease. I like to store shoes on flat solid shoe racks[18] or closet shelves, out of the boxes.

If you are short on space, you can get creative without installing a closet system by:

- Using stackable shoe shelves, shoe cubbies, or shoe cabinets[19-21]
- Stacking pantry bins with an open front[22]
- Using an over the door shoe organizer[23]

Whatever you do, please let go of the cardboard shoe boxes that your shoes came in. They take up prime real estate, and I have a strong aversion to cardboard (as you now know).

Certain types of shoes warrant certain storage, and I share a few of them below.

## Sneakers:

In my experience, people tend to have more sneakers than they actually wear. It's important to go through this specific category and keep only the items you use, that are in good condition, and that fit properly.

> This does not apply to "Sneaker Heads," true aficionados and collectors of special, rare, and often expensive sneakers. One of my clients is a Sneaker Head, and for him collecting, selling, and buying sneakers is almost a part-time job. In this case, it's more about the art of the sneaker, as opposed to the function. So for people who fall into this category, treat your sneakers like the art

that they are. Use acrylic boxes[24] to showcase your favorite pieces, or plastic storage boxes with front lids[25] for visibility and easy access (great for if and when you actually decide to wear them).

## Heels:

If you are tight on space, face one shoe forward and one shoe to the back. This not only creates more room, but also gives you visibility to both the toe and heel of the shoe. Whether they are strappy or zippered, make sure you are securing all closures. This will help keep the form of the shoe and it looks great.

**Pro Tip:** For those designer shoes that come with replacement heel tips and duster bags, store these extras in a decorative box or bin somewhere close to where you store your heels.

## Boots:

Store your boots on the floor, on a shelf, by hanging them on a rod (using boot shapers that come with a hook[26]) or by using boot stands[27] (which can hold multiple pairs). Make sure that you care for your boots by using boot shapers[28], these help your boots keep their form and help them stand upright.

Buying boot shapers for every pair can become expensive if you have an extensive boot collection. You can save some money and get creative by using rolled-up magazines, pool noodles, or the stuffing that comes when you buy the boots themselves.

If you are short on space, you can face one forward like with heels, or you can stagger them where the heel of the front shoe is nested in the instep of the back shoe.

## Sandals:

If you're tight on space, try keeping your seasonal shoes, like sandals or flip flops, in a plastic shoe box or decorative woven basket. This not only keeps them out of the way during the winter months but makes it easy to bring them out when it's summertime.

## Socks:

There are so many ways to organize your sock drawer. If you're like my husband when I first met him, then rolling them into a ball and stuffing them into the point where you can't open or close the drawer properly is your method.

However, folding into thirds and filing them upright in a row, like little soldiers, not only lets you see every pair but also helps maintain the shape and keep each pair from being stretched out. Use drawer dividers[5] to help keep the rows neat or use honeycomb dividers.[29] Have the fold exposed to achieve that perfect uniform look.

> I have a serious confession to make: up until very recently, my own sock drawer was an absolute disaster and the bane of my existence. Literally, it was at the point where I couldn't even open or close the drawer without pushing things down or moving things around so I could shove it closed and hide my little secret. I'm talking overflow. But I just left it as it was. The rest of my drawers are very organized. They are file folded with dividers, they are easy to maintain and the perfect example of what I try to achieve for my clients. Now, my husband's socks and my children's socks are all organized as you would imagine: triple-folded with dividers, color-coded by type. They look perfect. Mine, not so much.
>
> There's an old proverb that I love referencing when people assume that my house, my things, my closets, and even my socks are perfectly organized, color-coded, and labeled: ***The Cobbler's children have no shoes.***
>
> So, for whatever reason, I would go about my day, wasting time, and making my husband more frustrated when we are already running late, as he waited in the car for me while I tried to find a pair of socks that matched. Then I finally decided it was time to get my act together, that enough is enough. And I'll tell you exactly what I did: I emptied the entire contents of my sock drawer. We're talking stockings, ankle socks, low-cut no-show socks, ski socks, sweat socks, knee-high socks, my hand-knitted cozy socks I wear around the house in the winter, you name it. Everything came out, all the mismatched pairs and the lonely socks. This made me realize I had some lingerie and shapewear in there. Those things actually

belonged in my lingerie drawer, so I might as well go through that too. And then, low and behold, I realized that the deep drawer I stored my lingerie in was really wasting prime real estate. Lingerie is tiny, what was I thinking? So, I re-assessed the layout of all of my drawers and realized that with a little switch-a-roo, I could swap my bathing suits with my lingerie and make better use of the deep drawer. At this point, I figured let's just empty all three out together because why not make sure that the new home I'm creating for my socks is optimized and that the other two are nice and neat too?

By the end of this little project, I not only stepped up my sock game, but I also alleviated a serious amount of frustration; and I have already felt the impact on a daily basis. The satisfaction I feel when I grab a pair of socks within seconds is so gratifying, and at the same time also makes me feel a little foolish for waiting for so long to tackle this area.

Now, I bet you think this sounds like an arduous process that probably took me all day, if not longer. But by following the steps I have outlined, I sorted, purged, paired, categorized, and folded everything properly. With a little help from Andy Cohen and the Bravo Network, I finished this project while watching two episodes of Vanderpump Rules. That's less than one and a half hours (thank you DVR) of productivity while enjoying some reality gold.

**Belts:**

Men's belts are generally similar in buckle size and length. These can be stored on a specifically designed belt hanger[30] or rolled and placed in a drawer using smaller drawer dividers.[31] Women's belts of similar size can be stored the same way, using an acrylic belt organizer with individual compartments.[32] But for those with bigger buckles or wider belts, I recommend hanging them on a belt hanger or on a multi-hook rack behind a closet door.[33]

**Sunglasses:**

Sunglasses fall into the category of grab-and-go accessories. Keep them stored front and center with other accessories for easy access and make sure they are protected. You can get creative based on the number of shades you have and amount of space you have to store them in or on. You can store them in a deep drawer or on top of a counter or dresser using a divided sunglass holder.[34] You can use acrylic drawers[35] on a dresser top, or decorative tiered risers[36] on a shelf, or you can even opt for a display rack[37] like you would see in a retail store. The options are endless.

## Jewelry:

How much jewelry you own will dictate the best type of storage. I find that (similar to clothes) if you don't see it, you don't use it. I love to use velvet bracelet stands or necklace busts to showcase my favorite pieces on dresser tops. You can also use jewelry trees or stands for earrings and smaller pieces.

If you are storing your jewelry in a drawer or a jewelry box, the Stackers from The Container Store offer plenty of options to accommodate your collection. I love these because they come in an array of colors to fit your aesthetic and a variety of compartment types and shapes to accommodate the size and specifics in your collection.

## Scarves:

Sort these by size, fabric, and then by color.

Keep bulkier winter scarves pile folded or even roll the pile fold and place in a clear open front basket[38] or on a shelf. Keep these grouped in a zone with any other winter accessories, gloves, hand warmers, or winter hats.

Store lighter scarves together. Thin fabric scarves can be hung using a scarf hanger[39] or even a tiered pants hanger[40] on a closet rod. I like to file fold smaller silk scarves and place them neatly in a clear basket. You can also take a cue from the lovely ladies at *The Home Edit* and roll your scarves into a "doughnut." This is where you wrap your scarf around your hand over and over until you get to the end and push it through the hole creating a perfect "doughnut."

## Hats:

When you are organizing your hats, always try to utilize vertical and often unused space. If you're not sure how to store your hats, try creating a hat wall using decorative hooks[41] in varying heights on the wall. You can also use hat stands[42] on a dresser to showcase your favorites, or simply lay them flat on a top shelf.

Another creative way, that is especially great for baseball hats, is to use curtain hanger clips or hooks[43] which can hang neatly on a closet rod. I try to avoid baskets of hats, as usually the bottom ones end up forgotten. Remember, it's all about visibility.

**Seasonal Clothes:**

My ultimate goal is to be able to keep all seasons of clothes in the closet, but this is almost always impossible. If you are limited with space, consider having a seasonal drawer or shelf that you can swap out as the weather changes. Think tank tops and shorts in the summer and thermals and turtlenecks in the winter. Keep a bin (or bins) that you store your out-of-season clothes in. Store this bin in another area, like an attic or under the bed, until it's time to make the changeover. I suggest storing them in an airtight bin to help preserve them and prevent the attack of the moths. Take the time to review your clothes when the weather changes and you make the switch—it's a great time to edit your wardrobe of things that you want to let go of or donate.

## The Nightstand

By keeping your nightstand relatively clear, you are on your way to creating an environment that will help provide a great night sleep and foster good sleeping habits. Try to avoid using your nightstand as a catch-all.

What to keep on your nightstand:

- A lamp
- An alarm clock
- A small photo
- A water carafe

If you have drawers in your nightstand, keep the below items organized using drawer organizers or dividers:

- A book (or two max) – there is no need to keep your library or a pile of the last five books you read, or five books you plan on reading. Keep it to a minimum to provide a clean surface or organized drawer space.
- Lotion and/or lip balm.
- Eyeglasses and/or eye drops (if needed).
- Any medical devices you need to sleep.

What to keep off your nightstand:

**Cell Phones:**

Experts agree that storing your phone next to you while you sleep can be problematic for your health and your mind. Not only do our devices emit harsh electromagnetic radiation, but the blue light is also known to throw off our circadian rhythm and the natural production and release of melatonin before we fall asleep.

In addition, keeping the phone so close also leads to late-night phone calls, texts, or scrolling through TikTok. A better thing to do is to store your phone on the other side of the room, but if you must have it next to you while you sleep, keep it in airplane mode or simply turn it off.

**Food:**

Breakfast in bed, while it sounds nice, can get a little messy. Avoid the crumbs by keeping food out of your bedroom, off your nightstand, and in the kitchen where it belongs. Eating before bed is also known to contribute to poor sleep, indigestion, and slowing your metabolism.

**Paperwork or General Clutter:**

A cluttered mind and a cluttered nightstand will keep you from quality sleep. Keeping work or random items (contents from your pockets, bills, etc.), next to you at the end of the day can add stress and worry and keep your mind active and racing when it should be winding down.

**Humidifier:**

While they help produce a mist that moisturizes the air and can help your breathing while you sleep, having one close to you can be counterintuitive and keep you awake. Too much moisture is not good; these devices are recommended to be about three feet from your bed and usually on a higher, more stable surface. In addition, by being so close to your bed, you risk knocking it over or spills of (sometimes) extremely hot water.

**Bonus Tips:**

- Hang it back up. If you're like me and sometimes try on an outfit or two before making a final decision, you can have piles of clean clothes start to accumulate in the blink of an eye. Before they turn into what a client and now my family refer to as "clothes mountain," do yourselves a favor: pick it up and put it away. Clutter feeds on clutter. Save yourself the headache and address it asap.
- Big bins or tall baskets: I strongly advise against these in the closet or the bedroom unless they are being used as hampers.

  I once had a client who purchased about 10 hamper size baskets for her teen daughter to organize her closet. These bins are definitely roomy and can hold a lot of items, but having an organized closet is about creating visibility for your items. Unfortunately, once you start using them to store things, they usually turn into a pit of despair, with items never to be seen again—or at least forgotten about. When in doubt, opt for shallower bins with open fronts or windows.

 Take a picture! #igotdeecluttered

## Favorite Products:

- [1] Amazon Basics Slim, Velvet, Non-Slip Suit Clothes Hangers, Amazon
- [2] Quality Hangers Slim Plastic Hangers for Clothes, Amazon
- [3] Homeitusa, Natural Wood Clothes Hangers, Target

- [4] Cedar Space Cedar Blocks for Clothes Storage, Amazon
- [5] 4" Dream Drawer Organizers, The Container Store
- [6] Marie Kondo Hikidashi Drawer Organizers, The Container Store
- [7] Better Homes & Gardens Bamboo Adjustable Drawer Dividers, Walmart
- [8] CY craft Acrylic Shelf Dividers for Closets, Amazon
- [9] ROUFA Clear Acrylic Shelf Dividers, Adjustable Closet Organizer, Amazon
- [10] Closet Dividers for Hanging Clothes, Amazon
- [11] mDesign Plastic Divided Purse Storage Organizer, Target
- [12] Luxe Acrylic Handbag Display Stand, The Container Store
- [13] Cambridge Drop-Front Sweater Box, The Container Store
- [14] Wiosi Handbag Hanger, Amazon
- [15] Purse Insert Pillows Set by Fabrinique, Amazon
- [16] SONGMICS 3-Tier Shoe Rack Storage, Amazon
- [17] Room Essentials Clear Storage Box White, Target
- [18] 3-Tier Mesh Entryway Shoe Storage W/ Wood Top Graphite, The Container Store
- [19] Open Spaces Entryway Rack, Open Spaces
- [20] HEMNES Shoe cabinet, IKEA
- [21] Anbuy Shoe Cabinet, Free Standing Tipping Bucket Entryway Shoes, Amazon
- [22] Squared Away Eco Open-Front Stacking Storage Bin, Bed Bath & Beyond
- [23] Mainstays 12-Tier Over The Door Shoe Rack, Walmart
- [24] OnDisplay Luxury Acrylic Shoe Box, Amazon
- [25] BTMWAY Transparent Plastic Stackable Shoe Storage, Walmart
- [26] Tall Grey Boot Shapers, The Container Store
- [27] Whitmor 3 Pair Boot Rack, Amazon
- [28] Moneysworth & Best Deluxe Boot Shaper, Amazon
- [29] 32-Compartment Drawer Organizer, The Container Store
- [30] Simply Essential Non-Slip Belt Hangers in Black, Bed Bath & Beyond

- [31] Household Essentials Drawer Organizer Box, Amazon
- [32] Femeli Acrylic Belt Organizer, Amazon
- [33] Umbra Estique 14-Hook Over The Door Rack, Bloomingdales
- [34] Stackers Classic Lidded Eyewear Storage Box, The Container Store
- [35] STORi Audrey Stackable Plastic Organizer, Amazon
- [36] MineSign Sunglasses Organizer, Amazon
- [37] Juvale Sunglasses Wooden Display Stand, Target
- [38] Brightroom All Purpose Open Front Storage Bin, Target
- [39] Interdesign Hanging Organizer, Wayfair
- [40] Brightroom 5 Tier Pants Hanger
- [41] Essentra Home White and Gray Marble Wall Mounted Coat Hooks, Amazon
- [42] General Adjustable Hat Display Stand, Amazon
- [43] Mkono Hat Rack for wall, Amazon or Lunies Hat Rack for Wall, Amazon

CHAPTER 7:

# Children's Bedrooms

It's so important to organize your children's space in a transient way with room to grow into. As their clothes get bigger and their interests change, you'll want a system that can grow with them too.

Disclaimer: I have two small children, currently seven and four years old. So I have a lot of tips and tricks to help get little ones involved and excited about organizing. Don't get me wrong, my children are children. I sometimes hear the groans, and see the slouched shoulders and pouty lips when it's time to clean up. Toys are sometimes everywhere, and the place often looks like a bomb exploded. But they understand that giving away their used toys or clothes to someone less fortunate is an act of kindness, and they know how to put their dishes, backpacks, coats, and toys away. And even if they're reluctant to get the job done, they get excited and proud of themselves when they clean their room or organize their things.

Now, I find that there are a lot of children out there just like mine, but I also know that it's not that common. So what I'll do is share some of my tips and little secrets I use to get them involved. And if you have little ones, maybe it will work with them. And maybe not. But if your children *aren't* involved, hopefully I'll be able to offer some new tricks that may turn the tide for you.

## Letting Go

Approach their closet like you would your own. With children, it's easier to know what to let go of since their sizes change practically every year (or every three months for infants). But you're going to do the same four piles: Keep, Recycle, Donate, Relocate.

**Deciding Between Recycling and Donating:**

I never truly felt the struggle of being a boy mom until my son started walking and running. I never understood my sister-in-law, mom to my two nephews, when she would tell me that hand-me-downs would be at a minimum because of all the tears and grass stains on the knees. But sure enough, it has become my life. As opposed to storing or passing along all the outgrown clothes like I do with my daughter, my son's torn and tattered clothes that are beyond repair, go straight to recycling. And I suggest you do the same! Don't hold onto children's clothes with holes and rips and stains! That is unless you want to repurpose them into rags, or you have the time and are handy with a sewing machine and can patch those babies up.

---

*"Let it go!" – Princess Elsa*

---

Around the time that the summer is coming to an end and at the start of the school year, I like to overhaul all things children related. (We will get into school and art supplies in a later chapter.) As I've mentioned, this time of year always brings on more stuff, and to make room for all the new school clothes, shoes, and backpacks, it's important to edit and reassess what you currently have.

I like to enlist my older daughter in this process. She knows best what fits her and what doesn't. Truth be told, sometimes I hang on to a sweater or a dress because I love it so much. "Oh that dress that's two sizes too small? It can be a tunic! Leggings too small?! Guess what? We got capris!" But she knows if it is too tight in the arms or high in the crotch.

Even my son and other toddlers can recognize if the clothes are too tight, and empowering them to make the call if a shirt or pants are too small for them gives them such pride! Give it a try. And by showing them where the labeled bin for outgrown clothes is, they can take care of putting it away themselves!

Which brings me to…

The bin: **Keep a basket or bin on hand for clothes that are too small** so that you can donate or store for other siblings as it gets filled. You can also keep a basket or bin of clothes that are too big and they will grow into. Just make sure to label by age or size so that you don't forget and miss the stage entirely.

## Layout and Zones

Categorize all items you are keeping and create piles of similar clothes. It is important to create a zone for everyday use items within arm's reach if possible. As much as we don't want them to grow up, storing the things they wear daily at their level helps build independence and encourage your little ones to get dressed and put away their belongings all by themselves.

For example, I keep my daughter's more formal dresses on a higher rod and her dress-up gowns and skirts on the bottom rod. All out of season clothes are categorized in bins on top shelves, and in season clothes are organized in dresser drawers for easy access.

If you are tight on space, as children's dresser drawers tend to be on the smaller side, consider optimizing vertical space using over the door storage.[1]

On the flip side, if you are lucky enough to have more closet space than your child needs for their clothing,

**Mom Tip:** Don't get me wrong, sometimes my children would rather be playing with their toys than sorting and organizing their closet with me. So on those occasions, I'll try to get them excited about all the new things they're getting for school (they love clothes just like their mommy), or I'll turn it into a game. I'll put on an accent and play a game of princess/prince and lady in waiting, and we must quickly pick out an outfit for the ball! "Oh my darling! We must get ready for the ball! Does this one fit?! Will this one do?!" Hilarity usually ensues. Accents always help turn up the theatrics and help the children get excited and more involved. But because I have gotten them involved in this process over the past few years, they are both more and more inclined to call out the clothes that don't fit them throughout the year and manage this step on their own.

optimize the extra space by storing some of their toys, books, or mementos that may otherwise clutter up their rooms or play area.

## Folding:

Folding children's clothes does not differ much from folding adult clothing, except that they are obviously smaller, and definitely have more sets, especially pajamas. I like to create little bundles so that sets are always together. I fold the pants up the same way I would file-fold a pair of adult leggings: in half, crotch in, then up from the ankles into thirds, sometimes fourths. Next, I take the top and fold the arms in on both sides, to form a rectangle. Then you take the pants and place them at the waist of the top and fold up until you have a little bundle.

## Sports:

If your children are involved in sports, keep all pieces of their uniform grouped together in one location. This eliminates the scramble when you're headed to practice or a game and, again, gives them some ownership and independence when it's time to get ready or put away their uniforms.

## Children's Shoes:

I like to keep a basket, bin, or cubby by the door (whether in the mudroom or laundry room or wherever your children enter and leave your home) to corral all the little shoes together. Again, it's all about fostering independence. If they know where to put them when they come off, they know where they are when it's time to put them on. You can store dress shoes or out of season shoes on a shelf using behind the door storage, or in a cubby.

## Tchotchkes and Keepsakes:

---

*"Parents just don't understand,"*
*– DJ Jazzy Jeff and the Fresh Prince*

---

Embrace the tchotchkes. Without fail children will, are, and have always collected little tchotchkes. Things that seem like junk or garbage to you are prized possessions to be guarded and protected at all costs in the eyes of a child. A great way to avoid ripping your hair out over all of the little gems or erasers or whatever tiny item your child picked up from lord knows where, is to embrace it. **Embrace the tchotchkes**. Use small bins for them to corral all of their important thingamajigs. They will, eventually, grow out of it. What you need to do is help them understand that these things have a home, and they can't be left about on the floor for late-night toe stubbing. Provide a few small bins for them, and anything that doesn't fit needs to be reevaluated—and probably thrown in the garbage.

Keep a memory box[2] for things that are really special that you (or they) want to hold onto, and keep it at the top or back of a closet. You can create visibility to things like earned Judo belts and outgrown ballet slippers by using a bin with a clear front.[3] Differentiate baby mementos from tween and teenage keepsakes by having designated boxes for them that they can grow into.

## Nursery

If you are preparing a nursery, *congratulations!* There really isn't any other time like this, when you will feel an overwhelming sense of love, hope, excitement, stress, and maybe just a little fear. And I'm sure you're getting advice (solicited and unsolicited) from every person in your life: every family member, every friend, every doctor, every stranger, every book or blog, from every angle. It's a lot to take in. I always do my best to try to refrain from doling out my own advice from my own experiences to expecting parents. Sometimes it's hard to bite my tongue, but since this technically is a book of advice… I will consider this solicited, and I will keep it brief and cap it at three points:

1.  As parents, we are always learning as we go along, no matter what age our child is or what stage they are going through. No child is the same, no parent is the same, so techniques, results, and approaches will always need some tweaking. Just remember, no one will know this baby better than you, so trust your gut.
2.  If you get unsolicited advice you don't agree with or want to hear, just say, "Thank you, I'll keep that in mind," and go about your day.

3. The Baby Brezza.[4] If you are planning on trying to breastfeed, more power to you. If that is not in the cards for you, whether by choice or by circumstance, and formula feeding is in your future, invest in this heaven sent product. Even if you breastfeed and find yourself switching over to formula, do yourself a favor and go out and buy this magical piece of equipment.

When you are completely sleep deprived, walking around like a zombie in the dark, eyes half open at 3 AM in the morning and you need to make a bottle for your screaming bundle of joy, you could either: a) stumble like a fool in the night down the stairs to the kitchen to heat up a bottle either with a bottle warmer or go old school with boiling water while standing in your kitchen painstakingly counting the minutes, possibly falling asleep standing up, only to truck back up the stairs to shove the bottle into the mouth of your wailing, screaming, precious angel baby, worrying if the temperature is too hot, maybe stubbing your toe, and cursing under your breath, or you could b) float out of bed, take three steps to your dresser where this extraordinary machine is plugged in, press a button and immediately the perfect temperature formula is dispensed into a perfect bottle and within moments your baby is silenced, enjoying the perfectly mixed nourishment they crave, and you both are back to sleep before you know it. You're welcome. You can thank me later.

Just like with older children, it's easy to know when to let go of certain baby items as they grow out of them, get overused, damaged, or broken.

While the process for decluttering your baby's belongings does not differ much from what we discussed in the sections on "Children's Bedrooms," the categories are definitely more extensive and detailed.

Below is a list of general categories for all things baby related:

| Categories for Baby Items | | |
|---|---|---|
| **Clothing** | **Pampering** | **Accessories** |
| 0-3 months | Diapers | Pacifiers |
| 3-6 months | Wipes | Teethers |
| 6-9 months | Changing Table Pads | Hats |
| 9-12 months | Swim Diapers | Shoes |
| 12-18 months | Diaper bag Refills | Hair Accessories |
| 18-24 months | Ointments | Sunglasses |
| Pajamas | Lotions | **Bathing/Medicine** |
| Onesies | Creams | Towels |
| T-shirts | Powder | Washcloths |
| Long Sleeves | Trash Bag Refills | Brushes |
| Pants | **Feeding** | Grooming Tools |
| Leggings | Bibs | Medicine |
| Shorts | Burp Cloths | **Travel** |
| Skirts | **Sleeping** | Bags |
| Dresses | Blankets | Stroller Blankets |
| Sweaters | Swaddles | Stroller Attachments |
| Socks / Booties | Sleep Sacks | **Miscellaneous** |
| Swim | Crib Sheets | Books |
| Too Small / Too Big | Padded Sheets | Toys / Tech |

The size of your baby, and how quickly they grow (mine were always one size ahead of their actual age) will usually dictate how many sizes of clothing you should keep in the prime real estate of your dresser.

I suggest keeping all diapering supplies on top of the dresser or changing table in decorative baskets or bins. We all know that the babies get the cutest decorative bins, but don't start with the mom guilt if you re-purpose non-baby bins for the nursery. Trust me, they won't know the difference.

All other categories and anything additional that you do not use multiple times a day can be kept in a closet, contained in either a bin or drawer, and obviously labeled.

Your baby will undeniably grow out of each size of clothing and stage of diapers before you know it. Enjoy every second. And if you are planning on having another child or passing their outgrown clothes down to a family member or friend, use weathertight bins[5] to store the clothes, and utility storage bins with lids[6] to store outgrown supplies or baby equipment.

If you are not planning on holding onto the items, and are ready to let go of them, make sure you waste no time and get them to the donation location so you do not start the process of becoming cluttered again.

 Take a picture! #igotdeecluttered

## Favorite Products:

- [1] Elfa Utility Large Wire Over The Door Rack, The Container Store
- [2] Bigso Oskar Box, The Container Store
- [3] mDesign Fabric Stackable Slim Shelf Storage Organizer Box with Window/Attached Lid, Amazon
- [4] Baby Brezza Formula Pro Advanced Formula Dispenser, Target
- [5] Iris WeatherPro Storage Box in Clear, The Home Depot
- [6] IRIS Stack and Pull Storage Bin with Lid Clear

*My father, age 20, at his Peace Corps. training in Hawaii*

*My mother, age 25, at the Jewish Memorial Hospital in NYC*

*My parents on their wedding day November 7th , 1970 at*
*Our Lady of Perpetual Health in Brooklyn, NY*

*My family: my father Gerard, my mother Petra, my sister Carolyn, and my*
*brother Christopher, in October 1985, one month before "The Accident"*

*My Aunt Lollie and Grandma Teodora in 1988 at one of our elementary school orchestra concerts*

*My parents in 1999 on a family trip to Virginia Beach*

*My college roommate Michele, the "Rachel" to my "Monica"*

*My family: My husband Stephen, my daughter Taylor, and my son Ryan*

# CHAPTER 8:
## Children's Play Areas

It's a fact that children have more engaged and focused play when playing in an organized space than in a space that is in disarray. They play longer, learn more, and have more fun. And they help clean up! Achieve that baseline so they know what their play space should look like when it's clean and tidy. Give your children the tools they need to be the best they can be.

I'm going to let you in on a little secret. Your children are completely capable of putting away all their toys. They just need the right tools. They never leave a complete mess when they are at school or daycare, so why should the rules be different in your own home?

Don't get me wrong. I'm not saying there won't be days when it looks like a bomb exploded or when you find yourself on your hands and knees sorting matchbox cars or LOL dolls. But getting everything in order will, without a doubt, produce an environment of happier children, less stress, more engaged play, and more independence and pride in your little ones.

## Letting Go

Children feel overwhelmed when there are too many toys, or when there is a mess. They are just like us. And just like us, they have a hard time letting go. But if you are going to get your children's play area organized, you will have to help your little ones understand the importance of donating or getting rid of toys they no longer use or need. Or you can do it when they're not looking. I discuss these and a number of different, somewhat controversial, methods later in the chapter.

But you have to do it. You have to take out all the toys. I mean all of them.

- Throw away all broken or worn out toys.
- Discard any games or toys with missing pieces.
- Donate any games, books, or toys they have multiples of, have outgrown, or do not play with any longer.

## Sort and Categorize

Nothing brings joy to these little faces more than when their stuff is organized, categorized, and labeled. Keeping supplies in small bins they can carry also helps encourage independence and gives them the tools for easier cleanup.

Use a separate bin or container for each category of toy, and be sure to label. You can get very specific and drill down to very detailed categories depending on the type and number of toys you have. But you want to **make sure that you have enough items to create a category**.

What you don't want to do is waste an entire bin on Thundercats when your child only has Lion-O and Cheetara. If you find yourself with a small amount of a certain type of toy, try creating a broader category of similar items that make sense to your child, like "Good Guys" or "Bad Guys."

Some popular categories and suggested storage solutions in children's playrooms include:

| Categories for Children's Playroom | | | |
|---|---|---|---|
| Category | Examples | Best Storage Solution | Additional Options |
| Building | Wooden blocks, magnatiles, Legos, tools and tool sets | Store inside of reach-in open bins | Use a three-tiered cart for magnetic toys |
| Games & Puzzles | Board games, card games, floor puzzles, boxed puzzles, board puzzles | Store in original packaging on a shelf using dividers to contain similar games based on age, or in bins with lids to corral all the pieces | Remove boxes and store in zipper pouches and file them upright using a magazine rack on in open all-purpose wide bins |

| Category | Examples | Best Storage Solutions | Additional Options |
|---|---|---|---|
| Dolls | Barbies, American Girl dolls, (including accessories, furniture, and clothing) Disney princesses, etc. | Store larger dolls in long reach in open bins or in larger stackable reach in bins | Store large accessories in individual cube bins and store smaller accessories in multi-section divided storage boxes with lids |
| Vehicles/Transportation | Cars, trucks, aviation, Disney cars, Hess Trucks, aviation, boats, trains and track | Store smaller toys in smaller reach-in open bins, store by category | For larger items store on an open shelf or display on a bookshelf |
| Balls | Indoor vs. outdoor, soft vs. hard, small vs. large | Store in sports storage baskets with wheels | Store in toy chests, toy boxes or hampers |
| Imaginative Play | Play kitchen and food, doctor sets, vet sets, tea sets, costumes | Store in reach in open bins | Mimic adult spaces by using things like a pegboard for tools or open bin for play food |
| Costumes | Masks, clothing, accessories, tools, weapons | Store on hangers using a clothing rack or a toy chest for dress up costumes | Store accessories in open bins or crates |
| Weapons | Swords, light sabers, toy guns, shields, bow and arrows, Nerf guns | Store using a sturdy hamper to store tall or longer toys, secure an Elfa track to the wall and utilize vertical space | Keep smaller accessories in an open bin |
| Friends | Superheroes, (good guys, bad guys), GI Joes, Little People, LOL Dolls, Disney characters, Paw Patrol, PJ Mask, Ghostbusters, Thundercats, etc. | Store in reach-in open bins, separate by character, type, or general grouping depending on how many you have | Use small bins s to separate each type within a drawer |
| Animals | Farm, sea creatures, pets, dinosaurs | Store using smaller reach-in open bins | Use small bins based on the number of toys in each category |
| Books | Board books, hard cover, paperback, chapter books, volume collections | Organize by type, age group, and/or color and store in cubbies, on a standard bookshelf | Use individual wall mounted shelves, spice racks, or magazine racks to display books facing forward which doubles as decor and creates easy access for favorite books |

| Category | Examples | Best Storage Solutions | Additional Options |
|---|---|---|---|
| Activity Books | Watercolor books, educational workbooks, coloring books, drawing pads, lined notebooks | Store in open file bins or a paper tray | Store in an all purpose bins in an art or activity zone |
| Art & Crafts | Paint supplies, Crayons, markers, paper, etc. | Store using a three tiered cart and corral supplies by category using cups or smaller bins | Use closed bins with lids for toys or supplies that need adult supervision |
| Stuffed Animals | | Store in a toy chest or trunk or in a deep hamper | Use a mesh net attached to a wall or a zip up bean bag chair to hide all the stuffies |

## Layout and Zones

I create zones based on the child's interests and set up the area to provide them open space to play creatively on the floor or a table. You should use a main wall for the primary storage of your child's MF'ers. Every play space usually contains some sort of reading zone or nook, but the other zones depend on your child's interests. Do they love to paint? You need an arts and craft zone. Do they play with trains or cars? Maybe you need an area rug with racing tracks on it, or maybe a train table. Are Barbies taking over your home? Maybe you need to designate an area or table for Barbie's dreamhouse. I like to use smaller circular rugs or area rugs to create designated areas of similar types of toys, much like a daycare or elementary school.

**Storage:**

The best type of storage will depend on the number of toys per category your child owns. By getting creative with space, like maximizing wall space and optimizing dead space in closets, you can free up room and create a home for every category.

Below are some tips on categories that should be grouped together and suggestions on what types of solutions work best.

- Store their MF'ers in the main area of the play space using a cubby system or low shelving.
- Remove all the bulky packaging.

- Categorize using open containers (like durable tubs, bins, or decorative baskets) and keep them at eye level or within reach for easy access. Bonus if containers include handles, which help children take out and put back easily.
- Mix and match the types of containers you use, but you can use uniform bins for each storage unit, by section, shelf, or row for a cleaner look.
- Maximize wall space: use floating shelves[1], bookshelves, and push pin boards to store and display art, books, or toys.
- Optimize dead space by adding additional storage drawers[2] or shelves to closets or corners.
- Use small bins for small toys. This helps minimize dumping.
- Use a multiple bin toy organizer[4] against a wall to create easy access to a large amount of smaller toys like cars, trains, or figurines.
- To maximize the use of the floor, use stackable open front bins[3] on the floor for larger categories and/or medium-sized toys like balls, trucks, or dolls.
- Use low open shelving systems[6], the tops of shorter bookshelves, or cubby systems[7] to display larger toys (like trucks, doll houses, or spaceships) that don't fit in or take up the entire space of most standard-size bins or baskets.
- Store supplies like arts and crafts or board games that you want to contain the pieces in bins with lids.[5] Keep these supplies or games that should be used under adult supervision on a high shelf or out of reach. Use clear bins so your children can see the contents, know what's inside, but are encouraged to ask for permission.
- Use office supplies like bookends, magazine holders[8], or file folders[9] to hold coloring and activity books.
- Store books by organizing them by type (paperback, board book, chapter, series), age group, or color. Use individual wall mounted shelves[10], spice racks[11], or magazine racks to display books facing forward which doubles as decor and creates easy access for favorite books
- Utilize a clothing rod or rolling rack[12] for costumes and dress-up.
- Use toy boxes/toy chests[13] for stuffed animals or as a dress-up bin for clothes and larger costumes and accessories.

- Use a mesh bag[14] or zip up bean bag[15] to contain excessive amounts of stuffed animals.
- Use a sturdy hamper to store tall toys like swords, bow and arrows, or light sabers.
- Do not use toy boxes, chests, hampers, or large deep baskets as storage for smaller toys. You will create a black hole for broken pieces, missing parts, and random objects.

*Some fun and creative toy storage solutions include:*

Three-Tiered Cart[16] - One of the most versatile storage solutions. These carts are mobile and compact, with designated areas and additional dividers for a variety of subcategories. Use this for magnetic building tiles, cars, hair accessories for dolls, art supplies, or a tea set. The possibilities are endless, and it can be stored in a closet, in the open play area, or in a small corner or nook.

Cubby Systems[7] - Cubby systems are great for maximizing vertical and horizontal space since they come in so many shapes and sizes. You can position them in a variety of configurations to accommodate wall space, televisions, or windows. They are great at providing a streamlined look. Using labeled bin clips makes it easy to transition or change out the contents of each cubby as interests change.

Utility Track and Hooks[17] – By mounting these tracks on the walls, you can maximize vertical space and store a multitude of items, like Nerf guns, by using hooks or art supplies by using pencil containers, to corral each category.

Magnetic Strips[18] and Peg Boards[19] - You can mount these strips on the wall or the side of a bookshelf to store matchbox cars or other metal toys to create a fun and easily accessible display. Use peg boards to display play tools or artwork.

Zipper Pouches[20] – Use these to contain puzzles or games without boards. Cut out the name of the game, toy, or image of the finished puzzle from the front of the box and use it as a label. Just be sure to include the instructions!

I had a client whose son was constantly taking random containers, (Tupperware, boxes, plastic bags), filling them with his favorite toys of the moment, and leaving them everywhere and anywhere, usually losing it in the process. So we printed a label with his name on it, stuck it on a zipper pouch, and now he uses that special bag as his daily carrying case. No more meltdowns over misplaced toys, and no more missing Tupperwares or random boxes found with action heroes and mini animals.

Long Open Bins[21] – Use for Barbies or other types of dolls. Use cube storage[22] in a cubby for bigger doll accessories like doll toys and furniture. You can also use modular lidded boxes[23] to sort and label each category of accessory for Barbie and her friends.

## Labels

If there is a place in the home where labels are the most helpful and almost necessary, it is your children's play area. For little ones who are still learning to read, use labels with pictures and words to help them learn and still know where things belong. I download pictures of games, toys, and characters and use them to create a label which I print straight from my Brother P-Touch Cube.[24]

**Pro Tip:** Just like in their closet, you can try to leave room to grow in their play space. By leaving some bins or shelves empty, you have vacant homes for new toys. By using neutral tones and sturdy structured bins, you can easily transition as they grow and swap out toys for supplies for their future interests.

## Arts and Crafts

If your child is into art the way mine are, and like me, you have overbought crafting materials in an attempt to keep them busy, then keeping all these supplies organized is definitely on your list to tackle.

When you are editing down and deciding what to let go from this category, be sure to eliminate all the dried-up, broken, and used supplies. But don't forget to also say goodbye to those items they are no longer using or supplies for hobbies that they have outgrown or lost interest in.

When you are ready to sort, use some of the following suggested categories:

- Painting – Paint, brushes, canvases, palettes

- Drawing – Crayons, markers, pens, pencils, stencils
- Beading & Jewelry – Beads, strings, looms, jewelry kits
- Construction Materials – Clay, popsicle sticks, pipe cleaners
- Textiles – Ribbon, washi tape, yarn, felt
- Embellishments – Stickers, glitter, googly eyes, poms, feathers
- Tape & Glue

Keep the categories broad and create zones in a closet, cubby, or shelf system. You can contain the subcategories in zipper pouches or clear containers within each larger bin, basket, or cubby.

If you strategically group each category, you'll be able to keep those materials that need to be used under the supervision of a parent out of reach (like glitter and glue) and the kid-friendly supplies at arm's reach (like markers or paper).

The three-tiered cart is a great way to keep all of their creative supplies in one central location. And having a designated child-sized table and chair provides a zone for creativity, crafting, artwork, or even eating snacks.

Getting the arts and crafts in order is not only so satisfying, but it's another way to help build independence in your growing children. I don't know about you, but if I had a dollar for every time I get asked for more paper or a different coloring book... Now my children are so proud of themselves

**Mom Tip:** Another task I enlist my children for is preparing our supplies for the start of the school year. I gather all the markers, crayons, and glue sticks from our arts and crafts area and set them on the table. I give them a few blank pieces of paper and put them to work. They check each marker to make sure they are not dried out and are in good condition. If they are in good condition, they put them back in their color-coded bin. If they are not, straight into the garbage they go. Next, they move on to crayons, and anything broken or dulled down to a nub goes right into the garbage. By the end, we will have our updated collection, and we can see if and where we need to fill in.

for getting it on their own, and it makes cleanup something they are excited to do because they know where everything goes.

**Children's Artwork:**

As a mother of two, I struggle with the guilt of throwing out some of their "works of art," and I know I'm not alone. But I repeatedly tell my clients and myself that it's okay to let go of most of what comes home from daycare, school, or summer camp.

There was an article I read a few years back in the Atlantic, titled "*Throw Your Children's Art Away,*" that really spoke to me. Mary Townsend said, "If it's the act of *making* the art that's useful and good for children, then let this part of the art live, and then let its results die." Yes! Let the art die! Now, I know that many parents are looking at me like I'm crazy, and that they don't care and are saving it no matter what I say. And I get it. And some circumstances warrant holding onto these "masterpieces" more than others. For example, when your child has special needs and some of these simple projects signify an indescribable amount of progress or hard work, or artwork of children of divorced parents.

> I had a client who had limited custody of his child, and so those art projects that came home on those few days he had his daughter were so special because he didn't get the pick of the litter when it came to what she made at school. So everything was that much more special to him, even things I may have personally recycled. But I didn't judge. We just created a proper way to store them: we made a memento box for some of the items he wanted to keep the hard copies of and designated a bin that would be sent out to "Artkive" to have a custom book made.

Over the past few years, many companies have been popping up that take your children's artwork and photograph them into beautiful keepsake books. I love "Artkive." Their process is simple. You can also try Plumprint, Scribble, or even take pictures on your own and use a program like Shutterfly to create your own book.

When it comes to your children's artwork, don't drown in a sea of construction paper doodles. I often refer to fellow professional organizer, Laurie Paula of Simply B Organized. In her thoughtful and witty book, *Hot*

*Mess: A Practical Guide to Getting Organized*, she gives us some sage advice on what to hold on to and what it's okay to let go of. Simply put, keep items that have their hand print, that have a story or drawing they did about a family member or themselves, or things that signify milestones like writing their name for the first time. Let go of worksheets, artwork that is just scribbles, or arts and crafts that a substitute teacher could have assigned them (like gluing pieces of cotton to a paper plate).

Trust me, they will be bringing home artwork for years. Keep what speaks to you, but just remember that when they are grown and flown, they will not know what to do with bins upon bins of arts and crafts from the second grade. Be selective, keep what really means something to you, and make sure it has a home.

## Cleanup and Maintenance

Get your children excited about their new space, and work with them a handful of times by showing them where everything belongs. Because, as I've said before, everything should have a home, and they should know where that home is.

Be consistent and patient. Your children will need some gentle reminding, and there will be relapses. Remember, the change may take some time.

---

*"Are you not entertained?" - Maximus Decimus Meridius*

---

You have to do what works for you and your family. But one of my favorite methods is making it into a game. Sometimes we set a timer and race to see if we can get everything put away before the buzzer. Or we play the Twister game (thank you, Wizard of Oz) where we have to get all the fill-in-the-blank (animals, cars, dolls) into the storm cellar before the tornado hits!! The storm cellar is usually the bin or basket they belong in. Works like a charm! My children even ask Alexa to play the clean-up song and get to work on their own!

My husband's method is to play a sort of doom and gloom song (those of you from the 80s, 90s, and even 2000s might remember the Undertaker from WWF), and once my children hear that tune they know it's "the garbage" song. They race around frantically to get everything put away as he staggers around like a zombie, playing the song from his phone, arms stretched out like one of those mechanical cranes ready to pick up anything and everything left on the floor. As I type this out, it sounds a little morbid, and some parenting psychologists may be shaking their heads, but I tell you, the laughter and fun that they have makes me smile and gets that room clean in no time.

And then I have a friend who throws everything away, whether it's broken or they've grown out of it or she's had enough of it herself. Boom, into a garbage bag and onto the curb when the children are at school or out of the house. And she says they don't even notice and are just excited and happy when they come home to a clean playroom.

My point is that there are many creative and fun ways to organize the space and get your children involved in cleaning up. But I admit a lot of the heavy lifting and quick clean-ups fall on my and my husband's shoulders, and sometimes other moms when we are cleaning up after a play date. But having it organized, with designated homes, and labels, makes it that much faster for my children, for me, for my husband, and all the helpful moms and their children, to get it cleaned up in no time at all.

Do what works for your family. Involve the children or don't involve the children, but just remember all those toys and all that mess will not last forever. Sadly, they grow up. So enjoy it while you can—even the mess.

Take a picture! #igotdeecluttered

## Favorite Products:

- [1] Gold Polished Shelves, West Elm
- [2] Elfa White Medium Drawer Solution, The Container Store
- [3] mDesign Plastic Open Front Wide Toy Organizer Bin, Target
- [4] Bratton Toy Organizer, Wayfair
- [5] Artbin Medium Open Super Satchel Clear, The Container Store
- [6] Eulas Etagere Bookcase, Wayfair
- [7] EKETStorage combination with legs, IKEA
- [8] Threshold Acrylic Slim File Box, Target
- [9] Acrimet Horizontal Triple File Folder Holder Organizer, Amazon
- [10] RiverRidge Home Kids' Floating Wall Mount Bookshelves, Target
- [11] CY craft Clear Acrylic Floating Shelves Display Ledge, Amazon
- [12] VOGUSLAND Dress up Storage, Kids Clothing Rack Wardrobe with 2-Tier Storage Shelf, Amazon
- [13] 3 Sprouts Toy Chest, The Container Store
- [14] Jumbo Toy Hammock, Amazon
- [15] Wekapo Stuffed Animal Storage Bean Bag Chair Cover for Kids, Amazon
- [16] 3-Tier Rolling Cart, The Container Store
- [17] Elfa Utility Storage Track, The Container Store
- [18] Heavy Duty Wall-Mounted Magnetic Tool Storage, The Home Depot
- [19] Pillowfort, Modular Organization System Pegboard Brown – Target
- [20] SUNEE Mesh Zipper Pouch, Amazon
- [21] Large Seagrass Bin Rainbow, The Container Store
- [22] Brightroom Bathroom Organizer Bin with Handles, Target
- [23] Short Medium All-In Modular Divided 15 Box, The Container Store
- [24] Brother P-Touch Cube Plus Versatile Label Maker, Amazon

# CHAPTER 9:

# Bathrooms and Linen Closets

---

*"Hey Mikey, you gotta go to the bathroom?" – Mouth*

---

Bathrooms are a great place to organize and have some quick and easy wins in your decluttering journey. There should be zero paperwork or mementos to go through, and expiration dates eliminate any guesswork when deciding to let go of items.

Because so many homes vary with their linen closet/bathroom setup, whether you only have a linen closet with zero bathroom storage, your linen closet is in your bathroom, or you are blessed to have both, we will look at these two areas as a whole.

## The Closet

Like so many other spots in our home, linen closets tend to accumulate much more than just linens. Sometimes, this closet needs to be the storage for more than just towels and bedding. Usually, it includes medicine, toiletries, makeup, or cleaning products that don't fit in your medicine cabinet or under the sink, utilities for rooms close to the closet (think vanity light bulbs or filters for a humidifier), and/or your bathroom backstock. Whatever you store in your linen closet, go through the process step by step, and determine which items you need to store in this space. And just remember that devoting the time to organizing this space will save you time and stress in the long run.

# Letting Go

When it comes to your linens, there are many theories on how often you should replace your sheets, pillows, and towels. Most experts agree that for sheets and towels, two to three years is the magic number, but this all depends on the fabric quality, how often you wash them, and how you care for them. For pillows, the time is a bit shorter, and replacing those every one to two years is recommended. Remember, out of all the categories in your home to donate from, towels and sheets are most widely in demand by the Humane Society or local animal shelters.

When it comes to products stored in your bathroom or linen closet, using expired face creams can lead to rash, acne, allergy, or even infection. Consider yourself warned. You should also consider letting go of the following:

- Eliminate old, smelly, or discolored pillows.
- Let go of lumpy, deformed, or uncomfortable pillows.
- Say goodbye to sheets for bed sizes you do not have in your home.
- Eliminate damaged, frayed, or stained sheets and towels.
- Let go of towels that start to smell after one or two uses after it is washed.
- Say goodbye to towels that do not absorb water the way they did when you first bought them.
- Decide how many towels and sheet sets your family needs. A good rule of thumb is to have two, but no more than three, sets per person. One for in use, one to be washed, and maybe a backup in the closet. Eliminate the extras.
- Discard face lotions and treatments past their shelf life. Most shelf life dates are stamped on the bottom or back of the container (we will get to cosmetics later in the chapter).
- Let go of any dry or smelly products, especially those with active ingredients and those in jars.
- Prescriptions and over-the-counter medicines are a different story.

I have heard conflicting opinions on whether or not medicine truly expires at the manufacturer's expiration date or if the shelf life is longer. According to Health.Harvard.edu, a study conducted by the FDA at the request of the United States military concluded that about 90% of over 100 drugs, both prescription and over the counter, were perfectly good to use even 15 years after the expiration date. The study shows that the expiration date doesn't necessarily mean that the medicine is ineffective or unsafe to use. While the potency and effectiveness of most medications remain the same years after expiry, some medicines are outliers, however. So if the date is years past and you need 100% effectiveness for your specific medication, it may be best to buy a new bottle or ask your pharmacist. I always advise that when in doubt, consult your doctor and do what you feel is best for you and your family.

## Storing Your Linens

As with other areas of the home, undershelf baskets are a great way to utilize vertical space. Use shelf dividers[1] or decorative baskets to create categories and keep things from falling over.

Store your sheet sets in the room where they are being used to save space, or you can store them in the linen closet itself. Wherever you decide to store them, if you have multiple sheets in the same sizes, you can buy different colors or prints to help differentiate where they belong.

Store each set together with sheet organizer bands[2], or for a less expensive option, use bungee cords or ribbon. I also learned a trick years ago from my Aunt Elaine of storing neatly folded sets of sheets inside one of the pillowcases, a simple move that blew my mind. You can use this method with the organizer bands for a beautiful look, or on its own.

Store bulkier and seasonal items like comforters, duvet covers, or quilts in space-saving bags in the back or top of the closet.

While I feel storing table linens in the dining room makes the most sense, sometimes this is not possible, or in the case of one of my clients, having a closet designated to table linens exclusively makes more sense. If you want to store your table linens in a closet or with your bedding, you should still store them based on their category.

- Tablecloths, runners, and table linens can hang on a closet rod using non-wire hangers to avoid pulls or staining.

- If you do not have a rod available, you can also choose to pile-fold them and store them on a shelf or in a basket.
- Dinner napkins are best folded and stored on a shelf or basket.
- Use smaller containers to organize all odds and ends, like napkin rings or place card holders.

**Folding Your Linens:**

There are several ways to fold towels and sheets. I am pretty particular about how I fold my towels. I fold one long end towards the middle, and do the same on the other side. Then I fold each short end towards the middle. (Allow a little gap where the ends meet to make room for one more fold). Then I fold the entire thing in half. *Easy, peasy, fold in threesies.* Stack them with the fold facing outward and raw edges toward the back of the closet for a neater and streamlined look.

You can also roll towels to save on space. If you want to give your space a hotel vibe, you can put your rolled hand or face towels on display using a decorative basket or tray on an open shelf or vanity counter.

I highly recommend searching for a video on how to fold a fitted sheet. It does not take long to watch, and after some practice, you will be folding like a pro. Trust me, the investment in learning this skill is totally worth all the time, space, and frustration you will save.

## Non-Linen Categories and Zones

How you categorize the items in your bathroom really depends on how much storage you have. A great way to maximize space in the bathroom is to utilize vertical space. Use undershelf baskets[3], shelf dividers[1], and stackable bins[4] in your bathroom closet, and use stackable drawers[5] under the sink. If you are tight on space, you can also use a slim rolling cart[6] that offers more shelves and places to keep things hidden.

Keep those MF'ers close by in your vanity drawers by the sink, under the sink, in the medicine cabinet, or on your sink countertop. Backstock in this area refers to those items that you use daily and are stored in the shower or on the countertop, but that you keep refills of on hand. Think toothpaste, extra toothbrushes, hair and body products, and paper products. Most of these items can be kept in your bathroom or linen closet. If you are tight on space, you can relocate some of these items to other locations. Cleaning supplies can be stored in a cleaning caddy[7] in the laundry room or under the sink in a guest bath. Toiletries can be moved and organized in stackable drawers underneath the sink, and paper goods can be stored in your back stock overflow area or on garage shelves.

Below are some tips on categories that should be grouped together and suggestions on what types of solutions work best.

| Categories for Non-Linen Items in the Bathroom | | |
|---|---|---|
| Category | Examples | Storage Suggestions |
| Bath/Body | Soap bars, body wash, shampoo/conditioner, bath bubbles or bombs, body lotion, hand cream | |
| Shaving | Creams, razors, aftershave | |
| Oral Care | Extra toothbrushes, toothpaste, mouthwash | |
| Nose, Ear, & Eye Care | Nasal spray, swimmers' ear, eye drops, stye medication, eye wash | |
| Allergy & Digestion | Antihistamine, gas relief, indigestion relief, laxatives | Store together in an open bin on the shelf in your bathroom closet or linen closet, in stackable drawers under the sink, or in narrow bins organized by group in your medicine cabinet. You can group multiple categories together if their contents are small. |
| Cough & Cold | Cough and flu medicine, cough drops, sinus relief | |
| Pain Relief | Aspirin, acetaminophen or other pain killer tablets, pain relieving patches | |
| First Aid | Band-aids, antiseptic, hydrogen peroxide, first aid kit (see list) | |
| Travel Size | Supply of frequently used travel products, hair and body, hand sanitizer, etc. | |
| Sunscreen/BugSpray | Lotions and sprays, after-sun gel | |

| Category | Examples | Storage Suggestions |
|---|---|---|
| Face | Cleansers, lotions, creams | Store on your sink counter or in your medicine cabinet, and keep back ups in an open bin under your sink |
| Hair Care | Hair masks, serums, repair treatments | Store in a divided lazy Susan, in an open bin under your sink, or using dividers in a vanity drawer. You can also use an over the door hair tools organizer on the back of a cabinet under the sink, or a free standing organizer on a vanity top to contain blow dryers, straighteners, curling irons |
| Hair Styling | Hairspray, mouse, gel, oils | |
| Hair Tools | Brushes, combs, blow dryers | |
| Hair Accessories | Hair ties, head bands, hair wraps, bobby pins | |
| Makeup | All cosmetics and applicators | Store in a drawer using dividers, or stackable makeup organizers on your vanity |
| Nail Care | Nail polish, remover, nail files, nail clippers | |
| Feminine Care | Pads, tampons, liners, wash | Store together in stackable drawers or open bins under your sink, or in a vanity drawer |
| Cleaning Products | Bath and toilet cleaner, disinfectant wipes, air freshener, bathroom garbage bags | Store in a cleaning caddy or open bin in bathroom closet, under the sink, or in a linen closet |
| Cotton | Balls, pads, q-tips | Store in decorative canisters on counter or underneath your sink, depending on frequency of use |
| Toilet Paper | | Store in toilet paper holder near toilet, and keep back stock in a cabinet or under the sink |
| Travel Bags/Dopp Kits | | Store in a drawer, open bin, or where you store your travel accessories/supplies |

# Other Bathroom Areas

**Countertop:**

Keep your sink clear except for absolute necessities for your daily routine like your toothbrush, hand soap, and if you have the space, your daily skin regime. Use a tray or catchall to keep these items nice and neat.

**Under the Sink:**

Refer to chapter 4's section "under the kitchen sink" for more tips and tricks. Just like in the kitchen, make sure you measure properly, factoring in pipes and any obstructions, and categorizing similar items together. Use clear drawers for visibility. Maximize height by stacking drawers.[14] You can also stack an open bin[15] on top of a drawer or two for quick access to taller items like hair brushes or hair spray. Lazy Susans[16] are also great for this same purpose.

**Medicine Cabinet:**

Keep your MF'ers and prescriptions or supplies used daily in a medicine cabinet. Refer to the above non-linen bathroom categories, and apply them in a more selected and curated way in your cabinet. You can attach skinny drawer organizers[17] with sticky dots to the cabinet to help keep your categories separated and contained.

**Bathroom Closet:**

If you are lucky enough to have a closet in your bathroom, I suggest storing your medicine in this area in addition to your towels and sheets. This is not your daily routine medicine, but your over-the-counter remedies, preventative medications, and a first aid kit.

**First Aid Kit Checklist:**

| First Aid Checklist | |
| --- | --- |
| Prescription medications | Sunscreen |
| Aspirin, ibuprofen, or other pain killer tablets | Insect repellent |
| Baby acetaminophen or ibuprofen | Sting or itch relief cream |
| Antacid | Calamine lotion |
| Thermometer | Hydrocortisone cream |
| Band-aids in a variety of sizes | Burn cream |
| Antibiotics ointment | Gold pack |
| Antiseptic wipes and/or alcohol prep pads | Electrolyte replacement |
| Gauze roll and pads in assorted sizes | Eyewash |
| Medical tape | Disposable gloves |
| Compression bandage | Tweezers |
| Wound sealing powder or Quick Clot clotting sponge | Small scissors |
| Moleskin for blisters | A pocket first aid book |

## <u>Cosmetics</u>

Getting your makeup in order is such a therapeutic process. When organized properly, cosmetics look so beautiful and colorful and provide a feeling of having your life together, so I always have fun in this area.

As a former Cosmetics and Fragrance Buyer at Barneys New York, (IYKYK), my makeup collection has been and will always be broad and extensive. It's just part of my make-up (see what I did there). I've always known the importance of having it organized, as well as the importance of periodically editing my collection to clean out expired and old items. Because I have so much and I'm always on the go, I love to refresh my collection. So, like so many of my clients, I had to call in the professionals.

Cue Jenn Dockendorf of *Jenn Dock*, a Concierge Beauty and Wellness Expert.

She is a veteran makeup artist and licensed esthetician based out of New York. She's done everything from television, red carpets, and commercial work, to private clientele, and celebrity makeup. She's also my personal makeup artist and a dear friend.

One of her services is a make-up bag *"DeeClutter,"* if you will. She sorts through your makeup collection, helps determine what no longer serves you, narrows it down to the best items, and helps you figure out what you're missing. She offers recommendations on products, or provides personal shopping for those new items, and then provides her clients with a lesson. She'll even help her clients learn how to properly use cosmetics they already own, as this is an issue many women have. What I love about her approach is it keeps your makeup up to date and relevant.

Whether you bring in a specialist like Jen (who can be found at www.jenndock.com) to help you, or you tackle it on your own, this process is so important. Many of us hold onto cosmetics past their prime when it's usually relatively easy and inexpensive to replace them. Expired makeup and treatments can breed bacteria and cause awful problems for your skin.

## Letting Go of Your Cosmetics

So when is it time to let go of your old makeup? For this, I turn to Bobbi Brown, world-renowned make-up artist, founder of Bobbi Brown Cosmetics and Jones Road Beauty, and an industry powerhouse. Over the years, I have had the pleasure of working closely with her on a number of projects, including her cosmetics and other endeavors. I asked her for her take on getting organized and how to know when to let go of your makeup.

"I really believe in makeup cleanliness to keep me organized," she says, which I love because she and I are on the same page. "I'm constantly discarding things when they get messy and old. One of the easiest ways to clear out excess makeup products is to toss anything that's been open too long to still be safe, clean, and effective." She shares with me some "rule-of-thumb life spans" for products once they've been opened:

**Cosmetics Categories and Shelf Life According to Bobbi Brown**

- Foundation: 1 year
- Lipstick: 1 - 2 years
- Lip Gloss: 6 months - 1 year
- Mascara: 3 - 4 months
- Eyeliner: 1 year
- Powder: 2 years
- Eyeshadow (powder): 2 years
- Eyeshadow (cream): 6 -12 months

**Cosmetics Storage:**

As I mentioned, organized make-up is like a work of art. In my perfect world, every woman with a make-up collection would have a vanity, adequate lighting, and enough surface area to house stackable drawers filled with all their neatly organized beauty products.

Personally, I love using stackable drawer organizers to contain the variety of palettes, pots, and tubes. Marie Kondo's collection of glass trays and drawers[18] is my absolute favorite. But you can get creative depending on what your setup is. Whatever you use, it's important to use acrylic, glass, or containers of any material that can be easily cleaned, as we all know that make-up can get a little messy.

Depending on where you store your cosmetics—in a bathroom drawer or closet—treat them the same way you would any other category by keeping similar items together.

- Sort based on type, keep the same product categories together.
- Use drawers or trays[19] to keep your categories separated and visible on a vanity, dresser, or countertop.
- Use drawer dividers[20] if storing in a drawer.
- You can use pen cups/glasses or taller vessels[21] to contain brushes or pencils.

Take a picture! #igotdeecluttered

## Favorite Products:

- [1] CY craft Acrylic Shelf Dividers for Closets, Amazon
- [2] ECOHomes Bed Sheet Organizer Bands, Amazon
- [3] Metaltex Undershelf Basket, The Container Store
- [4] Like-it Deep Modular Organizer, The Container Store
- [5] The Home Edit Stackable Drawer, The Container Store
- [6] Yamazaki Slim Rolling Bathroom Cart with Handle, Pottery Barn
- [7] Made By Design, Dual-Compartment Cleaning Caddy, Target
- [8] IDESIGN Linus 11" Divided Turntable, The Container Store
- [9] mDesign Metal Over Cabinet Door Hair Care & Styling Tool Storage Basket, Target
- [10] NIUBEE Hair Tool Organizer, Acrylic Hair Dryer and Styling Holder, Amazon
- [11] mDesign Plastic Divided Makeup Organizer Holder Tray for Bathroom Drawer, Amazon
- [12] Sorbus Clear Cosmetic Makeup Organizer, Amazon
- [13] Threshold Canister Acacia/Glass Small, Target
- [14] The Home Edit Stackable Drawer, The Container Store
- [15] IDesign Linus Large Divided Makeup Bin, The Container Store
- [16] IDESIGN Linus Deep Turntable Clear, The Container Store
- [17] mDesign Plastic 3-Compartment Bathroom Organizer Storage Bin, Amazon
- [18] Marie Kondo Ink Black Serenity Countertop Glass Makeup Collection, The Container Store
- [19] Design Clarity Large Makeup & Skincare Storage Starter Kit, The Container Store
- [20] STORi SimpleSort Stackable Clear Drawer Organizer Set, Amazon
- [21] Acrylic Makeup Brush Holder, Amazon

CHAPTER 10:

# Laundry Room, Mud Room, and Utility Closet

---

*"I have more than two grades of laundry, okay? There's not just clean and dirty. There are many subtle levels,"*
*– Peter Venkman*

---

For a lot of us, our laundry room, mud room, and utility closet become storage for things other than the conventional laundering, outerwear, or cleaning supplies. Depending on a few factors, especially where you enter and leave the house, these three rooms may be one and the same. And let's be real, these areas have the potential to become the junk drawer of the home because, if not organized properly, they can quickly transform into a catch-all for everything and anything to do with household cleaning, repairs, storage for our everyday or emergency items. That's a lot of stuff!

With some simple tools and easy categories, these spaces can give us that sense of relief when we enter and leave the house or when we are spending time cleaning up or laundering.

Because there is so much crossover in these three areas, we will address them as one location in some instances. If you are blessed enough to have more than a combo of these three rooms, enjoy all your space and go ahead and apply the process and tips to each room in your home.

Before you start letting go, you want to determine *what* will be going on in this space.

> What happens in this area?
> Will you be folding clean clothes in the space or somewhere else?
> Ironing? Sewing? Storing cleaning supplies?
> Will you be dropping off shoes, coats, backpacks, etc.?
> What else will be stored there?
> How much space will you need?
> Is this the only place for storing cleaning supplies, coats/accessories?

Once you determine what will happen in these locations, deciding what belongs there will be much easier.

## Letting Go

- Relocate anything that is not used in this space or does not need to be stored here.
- Discard any excessively worn rags or ripped towels.
- Let go of unwanted or unused items, like candles, pet supplies, and outdoor games or toys.
- Recycle any empty detergent bottles or expired products.
- Let go of empty cleaning solutions, dried-up glue, or expired room sprays or oils.
- Say goodbye to torn gloves, mittens, or those missing their pair.
- Throw away anything broken, like cleaning tools beyond repair, lightbulbs, or expired batteries.

Some general categories for all three spaces:

| Laundry Room Categories | Mud Room Categories | Utility Closet Categories |
|---|---|---|
| Laundry Machines | Jackets/Coats | Cleaning Products |
| Laundry Baskets | Seasonal Accessories | Brooms/Mops |
| Detergent/Bleach | Shoes/Boots | Dusters |
| Fabric Softener/Dryer Balls | Hats | Rags |
| Stain Removers | Sun Protection (Glasses, Sunscreen) | Tools/Hardware |

| Laundry Room Categories | Mud Room Categories | Utility Closet Categories |
|---|---|---|
| Sewing Kits | Sports Equipment | Home Repairs |
| Iron/Ironing Board | Workout Gear | Light Bulbs |
| Steamer | Umbrella | Batteries |
| Starch | Tote Bags | Candles |
| Laundry Machine Care/Filters | Lunch/Picnic Baskets | Flashlights |
| Rags | Travel Accessories | Extension Cords/Power Strips |
| Extra Hangers | Luggage | Fire Extinguisher |

## Layout and Zones

Before you start to lay out your zones for these areas, consider your family's activities. Do you have space to keep your children's backpacks so they are not flung to the floor as they enter the home? Or do those get stored in their bedroom or another area? Do you or your children play sports? Do you have a designated area to keep their equipment? Do dirty uniforms get taken off before they head upstairs or to the shower? Is there a hamper easily accessible to accommodate that? Once you determine what your particular needs are, it will be evident which zones are necessary to make your space functional and laid out in a way that will help keep it clean and tidy. Below are some general zones that can apply to the three areas:

- Prep Zone - Where you can sort and keep dirty clothes, a sink to pre-treat stains, and shelving to store cleaning supplies.
- Cleaning Zone - Where you store your laundry machines (sometimes one and the same as the Prep Zone), or other cleaning tools, this can also include where you hang dry clothes.
- Folding Zone - A surface space used to fold and store clean clothes or use an ironing board.
- Drop Zone - where you drop off items from the day, can include shoes, coats, keys, or umbrellas.
- Storage Zone - Where you keep additional items, either personal accessories or shoes in cubbies, or cleaning supplies in a cabinet, shelving unit, or attached to a wall.

# Storage

I find that in these three locations especially, there is never enough storage or surface area. Try to find creative ways to install or add additional surfaces, cubbies, cabinets, wall hung hooks or racks, and over the door storage.

These areas also become home to items like linens or cleaning products when other spaces in the home are tight. Be sure to use appropriate containers for each type of item you are storing in this space. Use wire or fabric baskets for linens, and plastic containers for cleaning products.

**Laundry Room**

- Keep your detergent, softener, bleach, and all stain removal products close and within arms reach of your laundry machine. Keep less frequently used items up higher.
- Utilize wall space by hanging things like ironing boards, or brooms, mops and other cleaning tools with long handles using wall mounted broom holders[1] or command hooks.
- Be sure to consider how you launder your items. By adding extra hooks, or a drop down drying rack[2] you can make space to care for your delicates. If you are short on space, there are options for over the door drying racks.[3] You can also install a hanging rod or valet bar[4] for garments to drip dry.
- Create surface area by adding floating shelving above the washing machine or you can install cabinets to contain cleaning products, extra rags, and other miscellaneous items.
- Use over the door storage[5] to store smaller items.
- If you are tight on space, you can use slim rolling carts[6] to hold things like detergent or cleaning supplies.
- Keep a small garbage or a lint bin to avoid garbage piling up or walking through your home with wads of lint.
- Keep a basket for dirty laundry and one for dry cleaning handy.

**Mud Room**

- Make sure you have a place to hang up coats as people enter and leave the home. Add wall hooks, or coat racks with ample hooks per person.

- Keep shoes and boots organized using shoe racks or cubbies.
- Keep sandals corralled in a floor basket or bin. (This works for children's small shoes as well.)
- If you have the space, consider installing lockers, cabinets, or individual cubbies for each member of your family.
- If you have space, add a bench to make putting shoes on and taking them off easier for everyone in your household.
- Keep an umbrella holder and an all-weather mat handy to keep your floor from becoming covered in snow, rain, or mud, both are helpful year round.
- Use over the door storage[5] to store smaller items.
- Create a drop zone with a message center for containing everyday items like keys, mail, and a message board with a running to-do-list.

**Mom Tip:** Use baskets labeled for each child (or member of the family) to store their seasonal accessories, like mittens and gloves in the winter and caps and sunglasses in the summer. If using stacked cubbies, keep the younger children's baskets on the bottom so it's in sight and within reach. And when hanging coat racks, consider installing them with varying heights to help build independence and give your children the tools to manage their own daily routine.

- Always swap out seasonal accessories, coats, and shoes to keep this room and area from becoming too cluttered.
- You can use decorative bins to keep things hidden and eliminate the visual clutter.

**Utility Closets**

- Maximize vertical space by using broom holders[1] for mops, brooms and dusters.
- Use reach in bins[7] for rags, microfiber towels, sponges, or other cleaning tools.
- Use caddies[8] to differentiate the different cleaning supplies and tools you need for your kitchen, bathroom, and other areas of the home.

- Use an over the door storage[5] solution for smaller and miscellaneous items.
- Use smaller storage or drawers to keep tools for minor household repairs, like a screwdriver, hammer or wrench.
- Use an all weather mat if you are storing large jugs of cleaning solution on the floor to avoid messy clean ups.
- Use open bins[9] for your MF'ers like light bulbs, vacuum attachments, and extension cords.
- Store batteries using battery organizers.[10]
- Keep an emergency kit handy for power outages and include supplies like a flashlight and extra batteries.

Take a picture! #igotdeecluttered

## Favorite Products:

- [1] LETMY Broom Holder, Amazon
- [2] Galvanized Laundry Organization System, Pottery Barn
- [3] Over The Door Drying Rack, The Container
- [4] Rev-A-Shelf Chrome Steel Extendable Designer Closet Valet Rod, The Home Depot
- [5] Elfa Utility Large Wire Over The Door Rack, The Container Store
- [6] 3-Tier Mesh Narrow Rolling Cart, Pottery Barn
- [7] Large Wooden Stacking Bin, The Container Store
- [8] Made By Design, Dual-Compartment Cleaning Caddy, Target
- [9] The Home Edit Stacking Pantry Bin, The Container Store
- [10] ENGPOW Battery Organizer, Amazon

CHAPTER 11:

# Storage Areas: Garages, Attics, Basements, and Outdoor Sheds

The garage is the Bermuda Triangle of the home. It's where things go in and never return.

---

*"You wanna go do Karate in the garage?" – Dale Doback*

---

Your first step, again, is to determine what your goal is for this storage space. Do you want to park your car in the garage? Is the space meant for seasonal storage? Is it going to be a workout room? Will it house all your outdoor equipment? Once you decide the goal, go ahead and start sorting, eliminating, and determining what items will stay in the space.

## Letting Go

Say goodbye to the following items that do not belong in your storage area:

- Damaged equipment, appliances, or tools
- Outgrown or unused sports equipment
- Old toys or unused baby gear
- Broken or damaged decorations or those you have not used within the past few years
- Outdated or broken electronics

- Expired chemicals
- Old or unused paint cans

Disposing of paint cans and other hazardous material:

- Latex and water-based paint is not hazardous and can be disposed of at your curb with the rest of your household garbage.
  - There are a number of ways to dry out your paint for safe disposal. In fact, there are a variety of paint-hardening products[1] out there that turn leftover latex, acrylic, and stains into solids for curbside disposal.
- Never put liquid paint or other chemicals down the drain or into the trash unless instructed by your local waste officials. You risk contamination and pollution to our environment.
  - This includes but is not limited to batteries, oils, pool chemicals, and household chemicals.
- Contact your local municipality for the proper procedure for your town or city's hazardous waste collection.

## Think Outside the Box

Your goal should be to get everything off the floor and out of cardboard boxes. Obviously, not *everything* can get off the floor, but you shouldn't be storing random supplies in all that Amazon cardboard packaging piled in the corner. In these storage areas, accessibility is important, so try to leave as much floor space available to maneuver yourself and/or your equipment around.

Which brings me to cardboard boxes. Whatever you do, get your belongings, supplies, tools, and belongings from your last move that haven't been unpacked yet and get them OUT-OF-THE-CARDBOARD-BOXES. Not only do you risk your belongings getting damaged from moisture or mold, but cardboard can also be the source of a moth infestation, as discussed earlier.

Remember, cardboard boxes are a temporary solution and not meant to be used as forever storage. You never know if the handwritten Sharpie marker label is old or new. Do yourself a favor: empty it out, break it down, and recycle it. Get yourself a bin and look at the difference. Removing cardboard in your storage area has the same impact as changing out wire hangers. It's transformative!

## Layout and Zones

As you are sorting and removing items from your garage, be sure to follow the steps and keep similar items together. Some general categories for garages and other storage areas are:

| Categories for Items in the Garage | |
| --- | --- |
| **Indoor Categories** | **Outdoor Categories** |
| Home Improvement | Lawn Maintenance |
| Tools | Gardening |
| Vacuum & Accessories | Leaf Blower |
| Utility | Snow Blower |
| Cleaning | Grill/Fire Pit Accessories |
| Pest Control | Lawn Furniture |
| Pets | Automotive Care |
| Entertaining/Holiday | Bikes/Scooters |
| Backstock | Strollers/Wagons |
| | Winter Gear (ski/snow, sleds) |
| | Summer Gear (beach/backyard, water toys, outdoor games, pool supplies and accessories) |
| | Sports (balls, gym equipment, seasonal sports equipment) |

Once you have sorted all of your items into categories, you will have visibility to how much of each group you have and can determine the sizes of bins that you need. Remember to consider the following when picking the type of bin you want to purchase:

**Open Bins**[2] – Use these for items you access frequently, like extension cords or gardening tools. Store these bins in prime real estate.

**Weathertight Bins**[3] - Use for items you access seasonally or that need to be protected from water, dust, or bugs. These items are great for storage on top and lower shelves.

**Closed Cabinets**[4]**/Dark Opaque Bins**[5] - Use to store items that you want protected from the elements or do not want visible or displayed.

Don't forget to factor in all of the large pieces of equipment and determine how much space they will take up. The lawn mower, the leaf blower, children's bikes… where can these live that are out of the way?

---

*"To the windows, to the walls…."*
*– Lil Jon & The East Side Boyz*

---

Make sure you're utilizing wall space. To be honest, hanging things on walls was always very daunting to me, and I find that many people get intimidated by the thought of drilling into the wall. Nothing is permanent. If you make a mistake, it's okay. A little spackle and some paint really work wonders. Utilizing vertical space is the best way to get these big items out of the way and to make your storage more streamlined.

Below is a list of some of the best storage solutions I love to include when designing a functional garage or basement storage area:

**Metro Shelves**[6]**:**

I use these in practically every garage or storage makeover I do. They are easy to build, come in a variety of colors and sizes, and are a great tool when mounting shelves to the wall is not an option. I love to use these for backstock or to stack closed storage bins. By organizing your backstock, you can avoid overbuying.

**Utility Tracks[7]:**

These are great for keeping your things flush against the wall and because of the versatility of what you can store on them: everything from beach chairs, sleds, bikes, lawn equipment, and ladders.

**Bike Racks[8]:**

You can mount bikes to the wall, hang them from the ceiling, or use a traditional floor-standing rack if you have the space for it.

**Broom Racks[9] or Holders[10]:**

Store indoor and/or outdoor long-handled tools, including brooms and mops and/or rakes and shovels.

**Peg Board[11] or Tool Wall[12]:**

Makes storing individual tools and frequently used gadgets visible and easily accessible. With a variety of sizes and styles of hooks, holders, and shelves, you can maximize wall space and keep your tools well organized.

**Multi-Compartment Organizer[13]:**

These are great for containing all the different screws, nails, washers, anchors, and whatever else makes their way into the nooks and crannies of your supply drawers and bins. I even take it a step further and label each tiny compartment so that you can remove the packaging and still know what is what.

**Slat Wall[14]:**

Hang loose items like beach accessories, awkward shaped tools, and fitness equipment.

**Wall Mounts[15]:**

Use for bigger items like sleds or skis.

**Sports Storage:**

The types of sports you or your children play will determine the best type of storage, but if you have any sports equipment, designating practical storage will save space and allow for easy use and cleanup.

- For larger balls, use a triple bin rolling storage bin[16] - basketball, dodgeball, soccer balls.
- For smaller balls use milk crates, paint buckets, or smaller baskets - tennis, baseballs/softballs.
- For hockey/baseball/lacrosse use a storage rack[17] - anything with bats or sticks
- For golf use a golf storage unit[18] - to store clubs, golf bags, and golf accessories.

## Just Say No

Experts agree that the following items should not be stored in your garage:

- Clothing and Bedding
- Temperature Sensitive Items
- Propane Tanks
- Fresh Food

 Take a picture! #igotdeecluttered

### Favorite Products:

- [1] Homax Paint Hardener, Amazon
- [2] Stackable Plastic Utility Bin, The Container Store
- [3] Iris WeatherPro Storage Box in Clear, The Home Depot
- [4] Curver Titan High Cabinet, The Container Store
- [5] Rubbermaid Brute Tote, Amazon
- [6] Uline Wire Shelving Unit, Costco
- [7] Elfa Utility Storage Track, The Container Store
- [8] Steadyrack Bike Rack - Wall Mounted Bike Storage Solution, Amazon
- [9] Holikme Mop Broom Holder, Amazon
- [10] Reliahom Broom Holder Mop Hanger, Amazon
- [11] Wall Control Galvanized Steel Pegboard Pack, Amazon
- [12] Pegboard Organizer Wall Control 4 ft. Metal Pegboard Standard

Tool Storage Kit with Black Toolboard and Black Accessories,
Amazon

- [13] DEWALT Tough System Tool Storage Organizer, Amazon
- [14] Gladiator GearWall Panels, Amazon
- [15] HUPBIPY Garage Hooks, Amazon
- [16] Heavy-Duty Triple Storage Bin, The Container Store
- [17] Heavy-Duty Sports Storage Rack, The Container Store
- [18] Heavy-Duty Golf Storage, The Container Store

# CHAPTER 12

# Home Office

---

*"I have many leather-bound books and my apartment smells of rich mahogany." – Ron Burgundy*

---

The Home Office. Having it organized not only enables you to be more focused, but it saves time and money by improving your productivity and will absolutely relieve stress. And sometimes, adjusting the flow of the room and updating furniture can take an office from an afterthought to your favorite room in the house.

Whenever I'm organizing an office or a workspace, I ask my client to train me as if I were their assistant or I needed to take over their job. I have them walk me through what a typical day, week, and month look like. What items do they use frequently? What processes are they going through to get from A – Z?

What I'm doing when I ask that, is trying to understand how the space is used. What paperwork, tools, and supplies are used most frequently? What configuration can be made, what processes can be implemented, and what shortcuts can be created to make my client and their work more efficient?

And that's what you need to ask yourself. Take a step back and review how you are using your workspace. Look at your daily, weekly, and monthly tasks and how you execute them with a different set of eyes. Is there something tripping you up, or something that gets annoying because it takes so many steps? Do you use the same five forms when submitting a proposal, but each of those forms are in different locations? Are you constantly tripping over the cords to your printer?

Take some time to think if there are any ways you can streamline your processes to make your day a little easier. And consider what you need and what would be helpful in a perfect world.

Don't feel stuck in a routine just because you've always done it that way. Sometimes taking a step back gives us clarity to see something we ignored before. Sometimes it takes a different perspective to see the perfect solution.

If there really aren't any changes to your workflow that you can identify, that's okay. There may not be any, or you may uncover them in the future as you get your space organized.

## Letting Go

- Step one in an office is going through all the paperwork. Below, I discuss in detail how long to hold on to certain important and legal documents. But for everyday paper clutter, gather it all and take some time to sort through, recycle, or shred all the junk mail or paper that does not serve you.
- Discard any dried-up office supplies like pens, markers, highlighters.
- Let go of all the extra unused supplies and donate them to a school or office or someone who can put them to good use.
- Donate old unused books.
- Get rid of outdated or broken technology - keyboards, monitors, or desktop computers that you do not use or are not functioning.
- Transfer data from archaic tools like floppy disks or CDs.
- Part ways with that box of mystery cords you have been saving. Odds are that if you needed it by now, you have replaced it. The likelihood that you will be able to match up the cord with the device will be slim, and this pesky box has taken up too much space for far too long! (See my tip on electronic cords at the end of the chapter to avoid having this box return in your future.)
- Say goodbye to all the miscellaneous junk that has accumulated in

your drawers like pins, broken pieces, promotional items, and old business cards.

- Remove anything that will cause a hindrance to your productivity and is not office or work related. While it's okay to keep some decor and mementos out, you want to create an ambiance that increases efficiencies, not distractions.

## Layout and Zones

Creating zones, and having everyday forms, files, and supplies at your fingertips is so important in an office. If you use forms every day, use a stackable paper holder[1] to be able to take the form from the top. For all other files and paperwork, file them vertically to create easy access and avoid flipping through paper stacks. General zones in the office include:

- **Command Center** - Combine the next three bulleted items to form a sort of hub and drop zone, the "mudroom" of your office. They should be visible and prominent in your office, but they should not take up too much room. Use the wall or free surface area (ideally not on your desk or workspace) to create a command center where you will house your ingoing and outgoing mail and use it as a place for reminders.
  - **Incoming/Outgoing Mail**
  - **To do/Actionable paperwork**
  - **To be filed/Archive paperwork**
- **Desk or Workspace**
- **Files** - File cabinets are great when you have a lot of paperwork to store. When working from home, it's great to separate family files from business files. I like to designate a drawer per category or person. Even if household files are organized in the same filing cabinet as your work related paperwork, use dividers or separate drawers to differentiate the two.
  - Depending on the space and number of files you have will help guide you in the type of filing system that is best for you. They come in an array of materials and colors, so don't feel compelled to stick with the old-school metal ones we find in most boring offices.

- If you have a lot of files and ample wall space, you can use long filing cabinets. This will also create a nice surface area to hold paper organizers, books, or decor.
- If you have minimal wall space but a lot of files, you can opt for a taller single-row file cabinet.
- If you have minimal files and minimal space, you can use shorter cabinets with one to two small drawers.

- **Office Supplies**
  - **Paper Supplies** - Paper, Notepads/Notebooks, Folders, Dividers, Binders, Post-its.
  - **Writing Tools** - Pencils, Pens, Markers, Highlighters, Erasers.
  - **Office Tools** - Paperclips, Push Pins, Binder Clips, Scissors, Stapler, Staples, Staple Remover, Tape, Glue.
  - **Mail Supplies** - Envelopes, Stamps, Packaging, Packing Tape.
  - **School supplies** - Folders, Dividers, Binders, Pencils, Pens, Markers.
- **Printing Station** - Store printer and supplies, don't be afraid to store this out of sight in a closet or under a desk to free up space for a work area or other storage.
- **Charging Station** - Depending on how many devices you need to charge, this can be simple or extensive.

**Storage:**

- Make sure your desktop is organized with supplies you use multiple times a day and free from unnecessary junk. You can use stylish desktop organizers[2] and accessories to hold everyday items like pens, staplers, or paperclips.
- If you have room, or a secondary work surface, you can use file holders[3], paper trays[4], and additional desktop organizers to hold additional files and forms so they are within reach.
- Measure your drawers and use drawer organizers[5] to contain and corral all of your secondary supplies.

- o   Your top desk drawer should contain items you use often, but maybe not every day, like Post-It notes, push pins, rulers, or scissors.
- Maximize vertical wall space - use the wall to hang file holders, calendars, and push pin boards to highlight important papers and reminders. You can also install shelving to hold important books or decor.
- Consider the furniture in your office, and make sure you are using pieces that offer storage solutions. If your office lacks the space for a filing cabinet, look into desk options with these included. If you have closet space, maximize the vertical space by adding shelves or drawers.
- Remember, you want to use furniture or shelving to create extra surface area, but what you don't want to do is overcrowd those surface areas. By leaving room and space between desktop organizers, books, or decor, you can create function without all that visual clutter. DON'T FILL YOUR SPACE BACK UP WITH JUNK!!

## Paper Jams

Paper. There are so many opportunities to go paperless in the world today, but we, as a society, still hold on to a lot of paper. GO PAPERLESS when you can. The habit of holding on to documents that can be readily housed in a drive or cloud has never been easier to break.

With the legal nature of the next topic, I consulted with Joseph L. Linares, Esq., one of New York and New Jersey's top attorneys, professor, and public speaker, and how refreshing it is to hear that he advocates going paperless too. "The reality is that almost all documents can be digitized and securely stored without losing their effect. External hard drives can be kept in your home safe or safety deposit box and are easily added to. Other documents where original copies are often required," like those mentioned in the next section, "should also remain in safe keeping." But don't worry if your original is destroyed or lost, in most cases it just creates a headache, as Linares explains, "you can often get replacements through government offices and the courts, but that process can be daunting and time consuming."

*"I'm gonna go get the papers, get the papers..."*
*– Jimmy Two-Times*

A lot of the time, we hold onto paper because we are afraid that we might need it, like with manuals for appliances or receipts for big ticket purchases. But in reality, you can probably locate the manual to your baby's crib online faster than you can locate it in your home. Below is a quick reference guide for how long to keep important papers and when it is okay to let them go:

**Annual Tax Records:** Hold onto these records until submitting your annual tax return. You don't want to miss out on any deductions. Keep in mind that all of these papers can and should be digitized. Digital versions are fine, but start a folder on your desktop and email for "Taxes" and download the soft copies. Your accountant may even thank you.

- Annual 401k statements
- Paychecks and pay stubs
- Receipts for large tax-deductible purchases
- Records of charitable donations
- Stock purchases
- Medical bill payment records

The following need to be held for a longer term—at least seven years—the IRS often requires certain records, such as those below, to be held onto for seven years in case of an audit.

- Bank statements
- Brokerage statements
- Charitable payment receipts
- Insurance policies (until they end)
- Investment records
- IRS forms W-2 and 1099
- Power of Attorney documents

- Previously submitted tax returns
- Sales receipts (or until warranty expiration date)
- Tuition payment receipts

**Important Legal Documents**

Hold onto these records and files indefinitely. I discuss in Chapter 14 creative ways to store some of these files and other important home and family documents. For good measure, keep the originals in a safe location like, say, a safe! Just be sure to keep these in a weathertight or fireproof filing system. These are the things that really cannot be digitized:

- Academic records
- Adoption papers
- Birth certificates
- Death certificates
- Divorce decree
- Driver's license
- Durable Power of Attorney documents
- Employment contracts and records
- Marriage certificates
- Medical records
- Military records
- Passports
- Retirement and pension records
- Social security cards
- Vehicle and property records (or until sold), bill of sale, deeds, etc.
- Wills

# Electronics Cables

There are a number of ways to contain and hide those ugly cables from your office electronics:

- Cable management box[6] - These come in a variety of sizes and conceal multiple wires, including routers, cable wires, and power strips.

- Cable sleeves[7] - Wrap around sleeves to keep cables from getting tangled.
- Cable clips[8] - These help keep phone chargers and other USB chargers from falling off the desktop and into no man's land.
- Cable straps[9] - These can corral long cords for your devices, electronics, and even earphones.

## Digital Clutter

Instead of scrolling through Twitter or checking your Instagram, scroll through your own photos or email and get to work categorizing and editing them! You'll be surprised how quickly you can get through them. Here are a few things you can do while you're killing time, like when you're waiting at the doctor's office or twiddling your thumbs at the DMV.

**Pro Tip:** Whenever you get a new product that has a cord, take two minutes and label the cord. You can purchase specific cord labels for this purpose, but it literally takes two seconds to DIY. If you don't have a label maker, simply take a small piece of paper, cut it two inches lengthwise, about a quarter inch wide. Write on both sides what product it is for and be as specific as you can, i.e., "Ryan's tablet." Even though a lot of these cords are universal, there is nothing better than finding a cord with an initial gut reaction of, "Ugh what is this for?" but then seeing a little label indicating just that.

Email:
- Archive emails into categorized folders.
- Delete or mark emails as read.
- Unsubscribe from mailing lists.

Phone:
- Delete apps and app subscriptions that are no longer being used.
- Delete notes from your notes app that are no longer needed.
- Favorite the photos you want to keep for easy reference.
- Delete unnecessary photos on your phone, i.e., screenshots, duplicates, or blurry photos.
- Create folders of photos based on the topic the photo is covering.

If you're like me, you take screenshots of things that inspire or motivate you and that you want to refer back to, but then they live in the abyss of photos and videos. We rarely go through them, and usually never see them again or forget about them until it's too late.

I like to take screenshots of things that speak to me, whether it's something inspirational to help me be a better parent, recipes, craft ideas for my children, gift ideas for friends or family, or things that I want to buy for myself. So after I take the screenshot, I file it into one of the folders sitting in my phone's albums. What types of photos do you take? Some of the folders I have include:

- o Fitness (workouts and exercise)
- o Children's Activities (invites, flyers, info on their extracurriculars, or parties to attend)
- o Recipes
- o Shopping Guide (things on my wishlist)
- o Gift Ideas
- o Book Recommendations
- o Parenting (advice and tips)
- o Travel Hacks

- Create folders within your web browser by bookmarking sites you want to revisit.

Again, if you're like me, you have way too many web pages open.

Whether it's because we just open another app while surfing the internet or because we leave it open because we want to go back to it. All that digital clutter can cause stress and slow down your bandwidth. Just like with my photos, I keep folders of everything I want to revisit. What sort of things do you want to keep track of? My list is a bit more extensive than my photos. In addition to the photo categories, I also keep track of:

- o Party Planning Ideas
- o Organizing Hacks and Products (shocker)
- o Cleaning Hacks
- o Decorating Ideas

**Bonus Tips:**

- Make an effort to reduce the amount of snail mail you receive.
    - By going to Direct Marketing Associate's consumer website, DMAchoice.org, you can find out ways to edit the type of direct mailings you get from marketers.
    - By going to the Federal Trade Commission's consumer site, consumer.ftc.gov, you can find ways to opt out of credit card and insurance offers.

 Take a picture! #igotdeecluttered

## Favorite Products:

- [1] HeZone Paper Organizer Tray, Clear Acrylic, Amazon
- [2] Yamakazi Tower Deskbar Organizer, Bloomingdales
- [3] Blu Monaco White Wood Desk Organizers and Storage with Drawer, Amazon
- [4] Threshold White Wood Paper Tray, Target
- [5] Russell—Hazel Acrylic Drawer Organizer With Magnets, The Container Store
- [6] Yamakazi Web Cable Box, Bloomingdales
- [7] OTO Cable Management Sleeve, Amazon
- [8] Insten Adhesive 7-Slot USB Cable Clip Organizer, Target
- [9] VIGAER Fastening Cable Strap, Amazon

CHAPTER 13:

# Holiday Storage, Gift Wrap, and Crafting

## Holiday Storage

Whether you have decorations or supplies for just Birthday celebrations, or you have them for all the different national and religious holidays like Valentine's Day, Easter, Fourth of July, Halloween, Diwali, Thanksgiving, Hanukkah, Christmas, Kwanzaa, or Chinese New Year, be sure to store your decor properly in the off season by keeping them in a dry, temperature controlled location. It's a good idea to store all your decor in the same location and in order of occurrence.

Begin by gathering all the decor you have around your house and sorting by holiday. Once you see how much decor you have, you can determine how much storage you need and if you can or need to combine more than one.

You should be creating bins for each holiday and labeling them accordingly. As I always say, even a large storage bin should be organized. You want to avoid creating a messy bin of Lord-

**Pro Tip:** keep all miscellaneous holiday items, like craft kits you never got to make, seasonal decor you received as gifts, or children's artwork from years past (maybe ones you put up every year) together with each corresponding holiday storage bin(s). This way, when the next year comes around again, you are set for the holiday and have everything all in one place.

knows-what. I recommend using smaller boxes or bins to corral categories within each bin. This makes it easier to find what you need, and helps keep it from becoming cluttered again.

## Christmas Decorations

---

*"Dad, you taught me everything I know about exterior illumination." – Clark Griswald*

---

**Tree Storage:**

There are a multitude of ways that you can store your artificial tree. Just be sure to remove all the decorations and clean the branches before you tuck it away for the year. You can wrap and store it in either an upright bag[1] (which is the easiest but most costly) or you can opt for a horizontal plastic tree box[2] or fabric bag.[3] The most economical way is to use two 55-gallon trash bags, however, you run the risk of rips and pests making their way in. Ultimately, you want to keep moisture out and ensure the branches remain intact. If you go the "real tree" route, be sure to dry your tree stand thoroughly before putting it away for the year to avoid rusting.

**Wreath Storage:**

There are plenty of options out there depending on what type and size of wreath(s) you have. Whatever you choose, plastic totes[4] or fabric bags[5], I suggest letting go of the original box and avoiding damage from moisture and pests.

**Ornament Storage:**

Let go of any broken ornaments or ones that don't speak to you anymore. You can use boxes with adjustable dividers[6] to accommodate the variety of sized ornaments you have. For your more delicate and fragile ornaments, opt for a structured box with stackable and removable trays.[7] For those countertop or mantel pieces, opt for an organizer[8] with bigger openings to house all your large decor. Just be sure not to overcrowd each box, which can lead to damaging your precious decorations.

Personally, my family keeps our heirloom and fragile ornaments in a separate box. We even have a few that have little notes from the gift giver. One ornament in particular was part of a wedding gift to my husband and I from his late grandmother with a special message she inscribed to us. Having these keepsakes separated makes decorating as a family during the holidays that much more special and heartwarming. It gives us a chance to reminisce together about places we've traveled to and people we love.

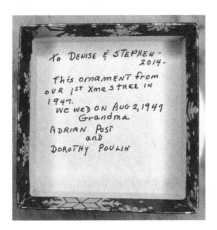

**Mom Tip:** By keeping a separate box of antique and sentimental ornaments, you can keep children from getting their hands on those irreplaceable keepsakes. Obviously, ensuring that these valuables are wrapped and stored properly is important. And as your children get older, the separate storage will be an added reminder that they have to be extra careful with these fragile ones. It's a great idea to keep notes or write the year on ornaments so that as the years pass, these little reminders spark conversations and provide a time to reflect as a family.

## Light Storage:

There are specific storage options with reels[9] that keep your lights from getting tangled, but you can also get creative by using a hanger and carefully wrapping the strands around in a figure-8, or by wrapping the lights around a wrapping paper tube. Simply slice a slit at the top and bottom to secure the ends of the string.

## Textiles:

Be sure to use weathertight storage options for your fabrics to keep things like tree skirts, linens, and pillows safe from mold and dust.

## It's a Wrap

There is a whole spectrum that people land on when it comes to gift wrap. Some people buy as needed, some exclusively use gift bags and tissues, some save all the gift bags and never use them, and some make gifting into an art form.

The goal is to store all your supplies to wrap and prepare gifts in one location. You can use all-purpose bins[10] to categorize gift bags and tissue paper, or you can get a fabric storage bag[11] designed specifically for gift bags. For wrapping paper, you can contain them in a tall garbage bin or hamper or use a similar bag storage[12] designed specifically for wrapping paper rolls. This one comes with additional pockets for things like bows, tags, and ribbon. Use smaller bins to contain additional items and label them by category:

- Ribbons & Bows
- Gift Tags
- Embellishments
- Tissue Paper
- Cellophane
- Gift Boxes & Tins
- Tape Dots
- Extra Tape and Scissors

## Crafty Devil

Among other things, my mother owned and operated "Queen Anne Fabrics and Crafts," during the 1990s in Teaneck, New Jersey. As you can imagine, there was an abundant overflow of everything from fabrics to crafting supplies that made their way to our home. So I know a thing or two about how the vast array of crafting hobbies, supplies, and tools can quickly take over a space.

Whether it's your interest or someone in your family who has taken up a new

I had a client who dedicated an entire wardrobe-style closet to her gifting supplies. I'm talking bins of every color, size, and fabric of ribbon, containers of faux flowers and embellishments, ornaments, tassels, and decorations in every color and theme. Then she had paper, tissue, and boxes, in every size, shape, and material. It was really a sight to behold. Let me tell you, her finished products and gifts really are works of art. But all of these supplies were practically taking over and falling out of the cabinet. So what did we do? We adjusted shelves, corralled loose items, contained similar categories in smaller bins, color-coded, labeled everything, and created a home for every type of supply. It made her process easier and less messy when it came time for the holidays, or when she's wrapping a present throughout the year.

hobby, your goal should be to contain everything before your hobby becomes more of a nuisance than something relaxing. It's amazing how many available options for storing everything crafting-related there are. There are containers made specifically for practically every type of crafting imaginable. Do some research; if you're into stamps, knitting, or scrapbooking, there are containers out there for all of the supplies and tools you need to be the best and most organized crafter.

A few tips for your crafting supplies:

- Do a walkthrough of your home, and gather all your crafting supplies. I find that these items tend to find their way across a home, especially when children are involved.
- Get rid of dried-out markers, glue sticks, and items you don't use anymore.
- Sort by item and then activity (or items you often use together). Keep more general and multipurpose supplies stored together in your prime real estate. (see chapter 8 under arts and crafts for crafting categories).
- Store in a location convenient for where you actually craft, if possible.
- Use bigger bins for appliances and tools.
- Use smaller drawers or containers with multiple sections for smaller materials.
- Keep messy stuff contained and hidden by using decorative boxes or solid bins with lids.
- Use a three-tiered cart if you have multiple hobbies.
- Like in an office, invest in furniture that can double as storage.
- Label everything so you know what is inside.

 Take a picture! #igotdeecluttered

## Favorite Products:

- [1] Elf Stor Premium Christmas Tree Cover, Amazon
- [2] Sterilite Clear Base with Red Lid Tree Box, The Home Depot

- [3] TreeKeeper XXL Expandable Tree Storage Duffel, Target
- [4] 30" Wreath Storage Box, The Container Store
- [5] Primode Christmas Wreath Storage Bag, Amazon
- [6] ProPik Christmas Ornament Storage Boxes with Dividers, Amazon
- [7] Santa's Bags Christmas Ornament Storage Box with Dividers, Amazon
- [8] The Holiday Aisle Multi-Use Storage, Wayfair
- [9] Santa's Bags Pro Install N Store Light Storage Reel and Storage Bag, Bed Bath & Beyond
- [10] Multi-Purpose Bin, The Container Store
- [11] TreeKeeper Gift Bags with Tissue Paper Storage Bag, Amazon
- [12] Homior Gift Wrap Organizer, Christmas Wrapping Paper Storage Bag, Amazon

CHAPTER 14:

# Keepsakes and Mementos

As I've mentioned, I'm a very sentimental person. I probably hold on to more keepsakes than I need or should, but like so many of you, I often fear letting some of these mementos go. Like I ask my clients and myself, "*Why* are you holding onto it?" Do you need to hold onto the boarding pass from your trip to Belize? Probably not. Do you really need to hold onto the wedding favor from an old friend who is now divorced? (True story, but you can imagine my joy when my client was happy to part ways with this unnecessary treasure.)

Oftentimes, people hold onto these little things to remember the good times, to give them a "Remember this? I can't believe you saved it!" feel-good moment, and they think it's so small so what's the harm. But the harm is that all these little things add up, clutter your space, and clutter your mind.

So my best advice when you are holding onto something is this: is there another object or picture that holds a deeper significance of this memory? If not, will a picture of this memento be enough of a reminder of the moment? Because if so, then it will probably take up less room than whatever it is you're holding on to.

But like I always say, if you can't bear to part ways with it, just make sure you have the room to safely and properly store it, and make sure it has a home.

Storage for our special keepsakes should be, well, special. If you are going to hold onto it, use a decorative box or sturdy bin with a lid. You want to avoid using baskets because these are memories that you want to preserve, and you should be protecting them from dust, debris, and the possibility of getting damaged. Take care of these items, and be sure to label them.

**Your Collection of Concert T-Shirts**

I find that most people have some sort of collection of T-shirts. Whatever sort of T-shirts you have an abundance of, whether they are from your favorite bands concerts you've attended over the years, your alma mater, your favorite sports team, or your trips around the globe, there are a lot of options out there to help you re-purpose them so they are not taking up coveted space in your dresser drawers. You can have them turned into a bed quilt using services like Project Repat or Quilt Keepsakes. If T-shirts are not your thing (maybe it's baby clothes or clothes of a loved one who has passed) you can have them created into a memory bear or stuffed animal of your choice, a pillow, or even a holiday ornament. Possibilities are endless, and the creative crafters at Etsy have a plethora of ideas waiting for you.

---

*"Jefe, would you say I have a plethora of pinatas?"*
*– El Guapo*

---

**Paper Trail**

Raise your hand if you have stacks and folders of papers associated with your children, certificates, programs, and pictures that you want to hold onto but find stuffed in random places in your home. I'm talking about report cards, class photos, sonograms, and your cardboard framed really expensive photo with the Green Knight at Medieval Times. These are special to us, we don't want to get rid of them, but we don't know where to put them. A simple and inexpensive way to organize all that paperwork and smaller keepsakes is to have a *memory tote or milestone box.*

By taking a weathertight file bin[1] and some letter-size hanging folders, you can create a box for each child or family member. These boxes will preserve all of the special documents, diplomas, hospital bracelets, pictures, and greeting cards you have amassed since you found out you were pregnant. It provides a folder for every stage, from pregnancy to college, and can be personalized based on your child's interests, religion, and/or activities. Below are some of the categories you can use or choose from, and of course, you can personalize your categories however you see fit.

You can get creative and label each decorative file folder[2] in a beautiful font with your label maker, or you can keep it simple with basic green office folders[3] and handwritten labels. Your call.

| Categories for Memento Boxes for Children | | | |
|---|---|---|---|
| Pregnancy/Birth | 6th Grade | Extracurricular | Awards |
| First Year | 7th Grade | (Custom Sport) | Sports |
| 1-2 Years | 8th Grade | Girl Scouts | Martial Arts |
| 2-3 Years | 9th Grade | Boy Scouts | Dance |
| 3-4 Years | 10th Grade | Scholarships | Girl/Boy Scouts |
| 4-5 Years | 11th Grade | Holiday Cards | Letters |
| Preschool | 12th Grade | Vacations | Birthday Cards |
| Kindergarten | College | Family Photos | Keepsakes |
| 1st Grade | Health Records | Holy Sacraments | Artwork |
| 2nd Grade | Medical Records | CCD/Religious School | Pictures |
| 3rd Grade | Report Cards | Bar/Bat Mitzvah | School Photos |
| 4th Grade | Documents | Bris/Baby Naming | Holidays |
| 5th Grade | Achievements | Camp | Miscellaneous |

You can also use the same method for your family's important documents. As we discussed in the chapter on home office, you can also use a filing cabinet or a weathertight bin to store these important files. Below are some popular categories that families keep as part of their essential files or "in case of emergency" storage.

| Categories for Family/Household Files | | | |
|---|---|---|---|
| Mortgage | Legal | Pets | Health Records |
| Loans | Will/Estate | Vehicles | Vision |
| Insurance | Certificates | Warranties | Prescriptions |
| Social security | Retirement | Manuals | Memberships |
| Bills/Utilities | Documents | Appliances | Photos |
| Taxes | Medical Records | Renovations | Cards/Letters |
| Children | Dental | Receipts | Miscellaneous |

**Picture This**

My photo collection is pretty well organized and extensive. I grew up in the era of waiting days, sometimes weeks, at a time for my roll of 24 pictures of film to develop from the local CVS. And I have actual photo albums documenting my childhood and youth. Being the third child, it goes without saying that baby pictures are minimal, at least compared to my older brother and sister. Truth be told, my collection of family photos has taken a beating over the past few years. From pulling out photos for memorials, wedding slideshows, or class projects and the like, I now need to go back and carefully re-assemble all the old albums and begin to create new ones.

---

*"Shake it like a polaroid picture" – Outkast*

---

Organizing your pictures is an understandably daunting undertaking, and sometimes it takes an event or momentous occasion to get you to start the project. Whether you are struggling with how to organize the prints or digital files that you have accumulated over the years, there are a number of ways to organize, compile and keep them safe.

Like you would with important legal documents, digitizing and storing your photos electronically is always a good idea. If you are working with actual prints, it's smart to scan and save them in an organized way on a hard drive.

## Letting Go

Being a sentimental person, I admittedly have trouble letting go of photos. And I don't know about you, but I am one of those people who take 10-15 photos of the same shot. I want options, people! You never know if someone is blinking, looking the other way, or if an expression may change. I'll take some standard photos, maybe a portrait, landscape, and then vertical. You gotta switch it up! And I'm telling you, if you were to look in my phone after an event, you would find A LOT of duplicates. Now, I do my best to delete the bloopers or "favorite" the best ones before I'm on to the next event, but sometimes they sit longer than I would like. And apparently, I'm not alone in this.

For all things photography in my life, I turn to Diane Fields Capozzalo, professional photographer and owner of Diane Fields Photography. With 20 years of editorial and advertising experience, she has worked with top industry creative directors, and has been featured in Martha Stewart Living, Bon Appétit, Vanity Fair, and Architectural Digest, among other publications. She also happens to be my sister-in-law. I asked her what her thoughts on the importance and best ways to organize your photos. "We find ourselves shooting multiple, if not almost infinite, options of any one singular experience," she says (is she talking about me?), "The need to properly organize our digital memories is more important than ever!"

That's why I love her advice to **edit your photo collection**. "If you're like Denise and take 50 images at one event, try to edit down to a handful of favorites and then print these memories," she says. "There's nothing comparable to a book of images or an old school shoe box that the younger generations can open up one day and relish in loving memories."

So take her advice and edit as you go. It will make organizing your photos a lot easier and less daunting. If you are having trouble with which print or digital photographs to edit, say goodbye to photos that are:

- Blurred or out of focus
- Duplicates (pick the best one or two)
- Damaged
- Bad exposure
- Memories you want to forget
- Memories that you don't even remember
- Negatives

**Categories**

While it may feel overwhelming when staring at boxes upon boxes of photos, or endless thumbnails of digital files, getting your photos organized is easier than you think. You can categorize photos based on any number of factors. Just remember there is no right or wrong way to organize your photos, do what works for you:

- **Chronologically** (By decade, year, and then month) You can also use eras or date ranges based on your childhood, college years, married life, etc.
- **Theme, Event, or Location** This is subjective, think "Birthdays" "Weddings" "Holidays" "Reunions" "Brazil" "Tennessee" "Italy" "Virginia".
- **Person** - by family member, or groups of people.

**Storing Printed Photos**

- Store your albums or print collection in a dry, temperature controlled location.
- Store individual prints in boxes or albums that are acid-free (or with acid-free plastic sleeves) so that the pictures will last the test of time.
- Use a pencil on the back of a picture to record the date so as not to damage the photograph. Ink can degrade the photo over time.
- An even better option is to use a filing card to record the details: the location, date, and people in the photo or album.

**Storing Digital Photos**

First, you need to consolidate all of your digital files and take inventory of your photos from your phone, on the cloud, or on other digital accounts. "I always advise friends and family to take those images off their camera memory cards and store them in external hard drives," Capozzalo advises.

Because of the metadata on digital photos, categorizing and organizing your files will be fairly easy, just as long as your camera was set to the correct date. If you are organizing photos that were scanned, keep in mind that the scan date will be what is recorded.

Choose how you want to categorize your files and keep in mind that you can drill down further than the three categories mentioned above with ease. For example, you can categorize chronologically with a date range, then by event, then by person. Your folder path may look like the below:

2022 —> Sports —-> Baseball —> Lukas' Tournaments

2022 —> Marcus Activities —> Cub Scouts —>Pinewood Derby

2023 —> Family Celebrations —> Holiday—>Sweet Vivi's Bakery Launch

2021—>Family Vacations—>Vermont—>Matthew's First Time Skiing

Another fun and easy option for organizing your digital photos is to create photo books using services like Shutterfly or Snapfish. You can create them based on the same categories as you would your files, based on a time period, an event, or for a person or group of people.

Just remember: **Always backup your files and prints**.

 Take a picture! #igotdeecluttered

## Favorite Products:

- [1] Weathertight File Boxes, The Container Store
- [2] Yaomiao Hanging File Folders, Amazon
- [3] Uline Hanging File Folders, Staples

# CHAPTER 15:

## My Favorite Products

I want to share some of my all-time favorite products that I incorporate into practically every job I have worked on and some of the creative ways you can use them.

Don't be afraid of getting creative and using storage solutions in unconventional ways or in spaces they were not intended. A lot of these products are multi-purpose, and if it works, then it works. For example, acrylic makeup brush holders make great storage for children's markers or colored pencils. Turnstiles or lazy Susans are great in the kitchen, but also for crafting. Below is a list of my top products and some of the creative ways they can be used:

**Elfa Over the Door/Door Hanging**

This item can be completely customized to fit your space and is great at creating little zones to corral smaller items or categories. It's so versatile it can work in any room and is the best way to maximize the empty vertical space behind a door or inside a closet or pantry.

- Kitchen: paper goods, linens, disposable tableware, oven mitts, dish towels
- Pantry: spices and oils, snacks, spreads, pasta, dried goods, drinks
- Bedroom closet: items like sandals, purses, hair styling, accessories, belts
- Children's closet: sports uniforms and supplies, hair accessories, diapers or underwear, bathing suits

- Toy closet: games, art supplies, blocks, magnets
- Bathroom: Shampoos, conditioners, towels, lotions, first aid, medicine
- Linen closet: lightbulbs, face towels, overflow products like back up toothpaste or medicine
- Laundry Room: detergents, cleaning supplies, sponges, rags, laundry softener sheets
- Mud Room: seasonal accessories, pet accessories, shoes
- Utility Room: batteries, flashlights, cleaning supplies, umbrellas
- Garage: small tools, extension cords, flashlights, bungee cords, painting supplies, gardening tools
- Gym: small weights, sweat bands, resistance bands, disinfectant wipes
- Multi-purpose closet: seasonal accessories like hats and scarves, crafting, gift wrap, cleaning supplies

**Clear Deep Drawer Bin**

This item is so versatile, it can be used in any deep pantry, shelf, cabinet, drawer, even your refrigerator. It is the best at maximizing these spaces.

- Kitchen: coffee accessories, small appliances, baking accessories, long cooking tools
- Pantry: canned goods, snacks, boxes of food, paper goods, condiments
- Refrigerator: cans, snacks, drinks
- Toy area/closet: games, art supplies, blocks, magnets
- Bathroom: toiletries, towels, lotions, first aid, medicine
- Under the sink: sponges, cleaning products, rags
- Linen closet: towels, cotton, backstock
- Laundry Room: detergents, cleaning supplies, sponges, rags
- Utility Room: candles, flashlights, cleaning supplies, batteries
- Garage: small tools, extension cords, flashlights, bungee cords
- Multi-purpose closet: seasonal accessories like hats and scarves, crafting, and gift wrap, cleaning supplies

**Three-Tiered Cart**

This mobile organizer is multipurpose and can be stored in plain sight or hidden in a closet or small nook. The tiers can be organized even further with small containers to hold a multitude of items.

- Kitchen - Baking station, Snack station, Bar cart
- Pantry – Canned goods storage, baking storage, small appliance storage
- Nursery – Baby changing station
- Toy Area/Closet - Store magnetic tiles, Wheel storage - cars, trucks, buses, doll accessories, Art station, Salon station
- Bathroom - Hair care station, Cosmetics station
- Laundry Room - Detergent/Cleaning cart
- Garage - Mechanic station, Gardening cart
- Office – Supply cart, print station
- Backyard - Bar cart, S'more cart, Summer toy/Bubbles cart/Chalk
- Gym - Workout cart

**Wall Mounted Organizer or Bin**

These small products pack a big punch and can be easily placed on walls or inside cabinets to maximize space.

- Kitchen: baking supplies, cookie cutters
- Pantry: food wrap, snacks, spices, packets, coffee pods, sweeteners
- Under kitchen sink: sponges/rubber gloves
- Bedroom closet: small accessories
- Children's closet: headbands, small accessories
- Toy closet: coloring books, work books, board games
- Bathroom: cleaning supplies
- Linen closet: cleaning supplies, backstock
- Laundry Room: sponges, rags, rubber gloves
- Utility Room: batteries, flashlights, cleaning supplies, umbrellas
- Multi-purpose crafting, and gift wrap

# CHAPTER 16:
## My Strong Opinions

I am always eager to learn something new and always try to look at things from another point of view. I always take suggestions and ideas from my clients when reviewing layouts together. I love collaborating and considering things in a way I would never have thought of. I love to read and scroll and look for new hacks and creative ways to accomplish everyday tasks. I love to evolve. I love to grow. But… having said all of that, there are a few things I don't think you can change my mind on. Let's call them *strong opinions*. You may disagree, but in my experience, these are my words to live by:

## Say No to Freebies

Think promotional items, T-shirts, water bottles, toys in a goody bag. I don't keep them, and I advise everyone not to keep them. While having children usually creates more of the freebie junk, adults are guilty of it too. Think promotional sweatshirts from your work trip or branded mugs. I had a client who had four or five suitcases filled with giveaway tote bags–just because they were free.

Just because something is free does not mean we need it, that we should hold on to it, or that we should take it in the first place. Before you keep that promotional T-shirt that you were so lucky to catch as it was shot out of a cannon from half-court by a cheerleader at a basketball game, really think about bringing it home. Is it going to sit in a drawer for years to come? Probably. Is it going to take up coveted space? Probably. You're better off handing it to the fan sitting behind you. Not only will you look like a generous hero, but you'll save yourself some time and space. And while you're at it, give them my card too.

Back to children and the tchotchkes… I've heard about the 24-hour shelf life rule for these sorts of things (like toys in a happy meal), and I love it. It's also been a great way to teach my children about the different value of things, how we need to take care of our important (usually more expensive) possessions, and that things like goody bag toys are made from inexpensive materials that tend to break easily. You may be familiar with the toddler meltdown when one of the dollar store goodies breaks within minutes of opening… I know I am. Enforcing this rule (we tend to keep these toys for a week) and acknowledging that these are not "forever" toys definitely has helped my family avoid these sorts of meltdowns and helps eliminate the junk.

## Double Trouble With Duplicates

You shouldn't have duplicates of categories in multiple places in your home. But there are exceptions to this: Band-aids, Scotch tape, pens, and other everyday items you use multiple times a day.

I keep three sets of Band-aids: one in my junk drawer for when my children have a serious wound (aka an invisible scratch that is only cured by the magical Band-aid), one in the master bathroom medicine cabinet for grown-ups, and one in the children's bathroom drawer (that's where I keep the fancy princess or superhero Band-aids that heal all wounds). I keep three sets of Scotch tape: one in my office junk drawer, one with my gift wrap, and one with my backstock.

Do what makes sense for your family, but really you shouldn't have things like batteries, stickers, stamps, or light bulbs scattered in different places, unless they are strategic, purposeful, and you know where they are. It's all about finding items more easily. When they are all in one spot, you know where it is when you're running low and when you need to buy more.

## Package Deals

When products come in double packaging, get rid of the outer ones. I'm not talking about cereal necessarily (although, like I discussed in Chapter 5 you can opt to decant cereal or remove the box, use bag clips, and file them in a bin), but for items like tampons, kitchen sponges, and granola bars, for goodness sake get rid of the outer box or plastic wrap and store those in their designated home. You will save so much space and time rifling through the packaging to get to whatever you need, and your storage will look better.

## Same Old Same Old

We are creatures of habit. Sometimes we keep things in a cabinet, or on a certain shelf, for a long period just because that's where it landed when we first unpacked it or moved in. Don't feel compelled to keep an item or items somewhere just because that's the way it's always been. Don't fear reorganizing a space, readjusting a shelf, or moving where you store an item. It's important to keep things in spaces that make the most sense and that offer the most convenience.

> I kept my Kitchen-Aid stand mixer front and center in my pantry because, well, it is big and expensive and a wonderful gift from our wedding. (Thanks Aunt Bunny and Uncle Tom!) But I use it maybe five or six times a year. However, my rice cooker, another gift from our wedding (Thanks, Aunt Kathie!) gets used at least once a week (#Filipino), and where did I keep it? Where else but the back of my pantry. I actually had to sort of twist my body and reach all the way in the back and practically move another appliance to get to it every time. What was I doing? But that's where it always was. Then a light bulb went off. And can I tell you how silly I felt? Me, a Professional Organizer. Learn from my mistakes. Don't fear change.

## Five Minutes

If it takes five minutes, do it now. I'm talking to you, a pile of clothes that accumulated when I couldn't decide what to wear. I'm talking to you, wrapping paper that was left out after last week's birthday party. I'm talking to you, a pile of schoolwork from the week that needs to be filed (or thrown away).

Whatever that little pile of stuff is, that little thing you see out of the corner of your eye when you walk past it to go to the bathroom, don't walk past it. If it takes five minutes, do it now. If you don't, it will accumulate, it will spawn friends, it will grow into a colony of clutter, and then you will really feel overwhelmed. Do it now.

## The Gifts That Keep On Giving

We all feel guilty about letting go of that gift that someone we love has given us. But I am here to tell you it's okay not to feel guilty! I know it's easier said than done. I tried to give this advice to one of my clients, and he laughed at me and, without hesitation, said, "Try telling that to my mother-in-law." But what I do share with my clients, and what I'll share with you, is that the gift was given, and part of that gift was the actual act of them giving and you receiving whatever trinket or item came all wrapped up in a pretty bow.

But—and even if you've never used it—it's okay to say goodbye to something that was a gift. It has served its purpose. It brought them joy to give it to you, hopefully it brought you joy to receive it, and it's okay if the life cycle of that gift has ended.

Do you think the person who gifted it to you would truly want you to keep it if they knew the stress it was giving you and the weight you were carrying holding on to it? Think of the space it's taking up in your mind and your home. Just know that you shouldn't feel guilty. And if they still come over asking where it was? Blame it on the dog.

## Childsplay

Get the children involved. Children love organization—they love structure and order. And they love games! When in doubt, make it into a game. Make it into a race against the clock, or a song, or against each other. I love a little friendly competition between siblings. And I love a little free child labor.

Which is why I love the sock game. It's part educational and part helpful. When I'm folding laundry, I dump all the unpaired clean socks on the ottoman or couch, and I yell out to my children, "Who wants to play the sock game?!" And the pitter-patter of feet and squeals just makes me laugh. Then, we either take turns finding a match or we race to see who can get the most paired. This usually depends on how much time I have to indulge them. We've been playing it for years, and I know their enthusiasm for it will probably end soon, but for now, I love that they love helping—and that I kind of outsmarted them.

## More Is More

It is possible to store massive amounts of your belongings in any space by being creative and thoughtful with how you organize them, as we've discussed in detail throughout this book. But remember, don't cram everything in. The best solutions *leave a little empty space.* They leave a little breathing room. You want your space to feel airy, and you want to keep it from looking stuffed to maximum capacity. In order to achieve that professional look, you need to leave a little space between containers, clothes, and dividers. It's about having more room, but not using it.

## Age Ain't Nothing But A Number

I think I have driven the point home that it's a great idea to get your children involved. The sooner you get them involved, the better. We started teaching our children from a very young age how to do things we wanted them to eventually do without hesitation, as second nature, like how to cover their mouth when they sneeze using their elbow, how to say please and thank you, and how to put the toilet seat down. But it didn't happen overnight. It took repetition, reminding, and patience. And the same goes for getting them involved with organizing.

By showing them how to do something, making it fun, reinforcing your pride in them when they get it right, and doing it together over and over with patience, you will set the stage for them to gain confidence, and to feel proud of themselves when they do it on their own. I'm talking about simple things like putting their toys back in a box, folding a shirt properly, or placing their dirty clothes in a hamper - all things my four year old son is an expert at. The sooner you start making these things a part of your daily routine with them, the sooner it will not feel like a chore to them.

But when do you get them started? I think by around two years old, your child is usually at the stage where they are able to start mimicking you. But while it's always great to start them early, IT IS NEVER TOO LATE! Your tactics may need to shift a bit, and your methods may have to include more incentives than just making Mommy and Daddy proud, but it's never too late.

I'm a firm believer that, at any age, we can make changes to who we are, how we look at the world, and the actions we take. Look at Oprah! She was fired at 23. Vera Wang sewed her first dress in her 40s, Ronald Regan went from Hollywood actor to Governor in his 50s, and *look at you*!

At whatever stage or age in your life, you are making efforts and commitments to yourself to make a change to better your life and the life of your family. You should be proud of yourself for that. As Alana Carvalho, licensed mental health counselor, author, and dear friend, so eloquently puts in her insightful and inspiring book, *Raising Empowered Children*, "Being self reflective—open to seeing yourself clearly and considering both your strengths and your areas for improvement and accepting yourself for who you are—is the greatest gift you can give your child." IT'S NEVER TOO LATE!

**Mom Tip:** Kids love to mimic Mom and Dad, or any authority figure who they look up to. They love to do "adult things," and what better opportunity for us to lead by example? Remember, they are sponges. They see you, they hear you, and they want to be just like you. So remember that, and let them see you doing things that you want them to do, like taking time to fold clothes, sweeping the floor, or exercising. Explain to them why you're doing these things: to help the family have clean clothes to wear, to make sure bugs don't come to eat all the crumbs, to stay healthy and strong. As parents, we are the most powerful influences on our children. I love when my daughter sees me reading and runs to get her own book so she can snuggle up next to me and do the same thing, "I wanna be just like you Mommy. Whatever you do, I'm gonna do." I swear it melts my heart every time.

# $hit Happens

I've said it before, and I'll say it again: life is messy. Your house will get messy. And it's okay! Whether it's a wonderful moment in your life, like welcoming a new baby, or a tragic moment, like dealing with the aftermath of a debilitating car accident, or you are taking a crack at writing your first book, sometimes our homes and keeping up with them take a back seat to something more important. And that's okay!

Spending time with our loved ones, taking care of our responsibilities, and doing things that are important to keep us happy and healthy should take precedence over washing our floors, folding the laundry, or organizing a pantry. But by putting functional systems into place, by setting our baseline, we make it that much easier to deal with all the things life throws at us. So let the dishes sit in the sink so you can play with your kids, leave the laundry in the dryer so you can go out on that date, order in pizza so you can take care of your sick parent. And take comfort in the fact that your home is organized, it's just on a break, and you have the knowledge and ability to get it back to your baseline.

CHAPTER 17:

# Staying DeeCluttered

I wish I could say that once you're organized the mess is gone forever and that the clutter never returns. But let's be real, we all know that we will continue to accumulate stuff for the rest of our lives. According to an article in the Boston Globe, the average American household contains over 300,000 items! And like I've said, there's always gonna be something: a project, a new hobby, the start of a school year, a birthday, where you are bringing more stuff into your house. What I hope I've been able to do is drill into your head that it's about putting in functional systems that help you maintain order in your home. Systems that will help you avoid getting back to a place of clutter and chaos.

And remember, getting organized—I mean truly organized—is a process, not a project. It's about going through *your* process, moving the needle just a little every day, and making changes that will help you for the rest of your life. As David Goggins, veteran, ultramarathon runner, bad-ass athlete, and author says in his book *Can't Hurt Me*, "[it] means digging down to the microlevel and doing something that sucks every day. Even if it's something as simple as making your bed, doing the dishes, ironing your clothes, or getting up before dawn and running two miles each day."

It's also up to us to be mindful and to really think about what we're bringing into our home. When you're out shopping and making a new purchase, big or small, consider how you will incorporate this new item into your organized space. Where will it live, and how will it be stored? If you are buying more of a staple item, like batteries, will there be room for it in your battery storage? Do you even need more batteries?

Life can get messy, both physically and mentally, and we all go through it, whether its work, ski trips, birthday parties, business trips, or sporting events, whatever keeps you popping in and out of your home, sometimes with suitcases that don't get unpacked for days, maybe weeks at a time. And things pile up. You may get stressed out by all the stuff that is everywhere. I get it.

I know you're thinking, "Your house is probably totally organized, labels galore." And you're right. For the most part, it is. ***But it's not all organized, all the time.*** I will admit, I am one of those annoying people that likes packing days in advance. It makes me happy to be prepared and ready to go, and I actually get a little anxious if I'm not. And I really love the feeling when I can unpack the second I get home. Is that strange? I can't be the only one. Well, strange or not, this is what I love to do. ***But it doesn't happen all the time.*** Sometimes, I don't have time or energy to unpack, and my bags sit for weeks. And yes, my house can look like a bomb went off everywhere. Not only am I the *DeeCluttered* President, I'm also a client. (See what I did there?)

And I get it, life happens. It happens to me, too, a professional organizer. Remember what they say about the cobbler, right? The difference is my home is set up with basic functional systems where ***practically*** everything has a home. And if it doesn't have a home yet, we know we need to create one for it.

Our home has a baseline. It's where I know, my husband knows, and even my children know, that it can and will get back to when life happens and the house gets off track. Because forget it, once Halloween hits my husband and I know we are in for a mess. Our home gets flipped upside down and back again for about three months. And I know there are so many families just like ours! Between hosting Thanksgiving, our son's birthday in December, and then Christmas and our daughter's birthday in January, it can get crazy. We have visitors, parties, and presents and, well, stuff sometimes doesn't get put away right away. It's chaotic to say the least, but still loads of fun. And sometimes the laundry gets backed up, or the mail begins to pile, or a monstrosity of toys have crept their way into the living room from the playroom, or there are new toys that haven't quite found their home yet. And let's be real, this can happen at any time of the year. There are always events, activities, and commitments that keep us on the go, sometimes leaving our home looking like a tornado blew through.

## Embrace the Mess

It's a little stressful until we get everything back to where things need to be. Sometimes it takes longer than others, but my husband and I can look at each other and laugh about the mess instead of getting upset or resentful about it. We have relief in knowing that it's temporary, and so we embrace the mess for a little. We just don't normalize it. And it's not easy to embrace it, but we try to because we know that it's not too difficult to get back to our baseline.

We aren't completely overwhelmed or physically affected by the clutter, and you shouldn't be either. So go get that baseline! If you have functional systems in place, cleaning up at the end of the day should not take too much time.

## The Sunday Reset

The process of getting prepared and trying to avoid the Sunday Scaries is not something new. Just like getting your home organized, resetting for the week is unique to each individual or family. Whether your reset includes self-care, home care, or just some quiet time to decompress, the goal of your Sunday reset should be to get your mind, body, and home ready for the start of the week. By getting ahead of some smaller tasks that cause big delays, you free your mind of stress and anxiety, allowing for a good night of sleep and providing the energy you need to tackle your week head on.

Resets can include whatever works for you and your family to feel more prepared at the end of the day: whether it's stocking your fridge, meal prepping, doing a load (or three) of laundry, changing your sheets, reading a book, meditating, taking a bath, washing your makeup brushes, or exercising. Even if you're not a planner and you don't keep a family calendar, do your best to list the events of the week ahead. Simply lay out events you want to remember, projects you want to tackle, or tasks you want to accomplish. By organizing your thoughts, you can clear your mind and avoid feeling overwhelmed or anxious going into the days ahead. No more Sunday Scaries!

We run the dishes every night and do our best to pick up the toys before going to bed. I try to get at least one load of laundry done per day, if there is time for two, then great. Otherwise it's playing catch up on the weekends.

Whatever you opt to include in your reset, the following steps are quick, easy, and essential to getting ahead of the game, waking up to a tidy home, and maybe just a little bit more relaxed:

**Step one:** Do the dishes and wipe down all the surfaces of your kitchen.

**Step two:** Take out the garbage.

**Step three:** Sweep the floors.

**Step four:** Set out your clothes for the next morning. If you have children, set out their clothes too.

**Step five:** Pick up any miscellaneous clothes, toys, or objects that are in the main living space that don't belong there.

Having everything prepared before you go to sleep is a great way to put your mind at ease. Knowing that you'll have a little more time in the morning to, perhaps, actually sit and have a moment to yourself is absolutely satisfying.

**Pro Tip:** dry the sink by wiping it down with a paper towel once it's been emptied and rinsed clean.

**Pro Tip:** Keep an empty basket handy, whether in the living room or at the bottom of the stairs, to corral all those random items that are left out at the end of the day. As my last step, I will walk through the house and collect everything into the basket and bring it up before I go up to bed and leave it to be addressed in the morning. You can even have a basket for each family member. Have them tackle this step by being responsible for whatever items are theirs.

*"What, like it's hard?"*
*– Elle Woods*

## Choose Your Hard

Now, I can't promise that this process will be easy because it may not be. But has living your life with clutter taking over been easy?

This process will be hard, but living a life of anxiety and stress because of a clouded home and mind is hard. Choose your hard.

Letting go of your belongings is hard, but being consumed by your belongings is hard. Choose your hard.

Making the time to sort and purge is hard, but constantly running late because you can't find everyday items you need to get out the door is hard. Choose your hard.

My goal as a professional organizer, and by writing this book, is to help give you the confidence and the permission to let things go, to guide you on your journey, and offer the support to make the process a little easier. And in the end, I hope I have been able to provide some tips and tools to help you realize that you can do it on your own.

I can promise that once you attack one area of your home, you will feel such satisfaction, pride, relief, and empowerment to continue to another area, and another and another.

There are a lot of things in this life that we can't control, so take hold of the things that you can.

My husband and I always say, "Nothing changes if nothing changes."

Now, take a deep breath, and go get started.

# Acknowledgments

Special Thanks to:

All my clients, past and present, thank you for welcoming me into your homes and businesses, and allowing me to be a part of your journeys and your lives. I appreciate you trusting me, my methods, and my process more than you will ever know. I have learned so much working with each of you and being able to bring some relief to your lives has been my real reward.

All my experts who took the time to lend their voice and their advice to this labor of love, thank you for your support and for contributing without hesitation, it means the world to me.

Everyone at She Rises Studios, especially Hanna Olivas and Adriana Luna Carlos. From day one you have been enthusiastic and passionate about me, my brand, and my vision. Thank you for welcoming me into the She Rises family, for your encouragement, your guidance, and your support.

Alice Pate, thank you for your ingenuity, your insight, your kind words, and your patience with me. And thank you for your love of movie quotes.

Renee Towell, thank you for seeing something in me, for taking a chance on an unknown, and for joining me on the ride. Your support and confidence in me have been invaluable, and I am grateful to have you in my life.

My girls, especially Ana, Danielle, Jen T., Jen Z., Pam, Michele, and Michelle. Thank you for your endless support, your love, and your laughter. My sisters for life.

My mother and father-in-law, thank you for all your generosity and support, but especially in growing my business, and in so many more ways than just helping me build furniture or watching the kids when I needed to work late, but most importantly for your love and encouragement. I love you both.

My Aunt Lollie, thank you for always being there for my father, especially during your years of recovery, for teaching me so many things like what uncouth means, for helping raise the three of us, and for all the love and support over the years. I love you, RIP.

My Grandma, thank you for dropping everything and being the loving mother to my mom when she needed you most, for showing me love, patience and pride in everything I did, for all the advice on our long walks, for teaching me how to make Balatung, and for helping raise all of us, my 21 cousins included. I love you, until we meet again.

My brother Chris and sister Carolyn, thank you for being there for me, for being my original clients and for supporting me from day one when I decided to go on this journey. Our childhood helped shape who I am, my love for organizing, and my incessant movie and song quoting, so thank you. I love you guys.

Mom & Dad, thank you for giving me everything I ever needed growing up, for all the selfless things you did and continue to do for us, for the sacrifices you made, for making me who I am today, for giving me the best childhood nicknames, and for always showing me love, support, devotion, and what family is all about. I love you both, always.

Taylor & Ryan, thank you for being the most loving and cuddly children a mom could ever dream of, for being my motivation to never give up, and my inspiration to be the best mama I can be, and for loving my accents. You are the reasons I never take any moment for granted. Remember your promise that you will never turn into bratty teenagers, and that you will always be each other's most important person. I love you both higher than the earth, heaven, and sky, no matter what.

Stephen, I am the proudest woman in the world to be able to call you my husband. Thank you for being my champion, for believing in me always, even when I doubted myself, for keeping me grounded, and inspiring me every day, for being the best support and greatest partner in this life together, and for picking up where I fall short - especially while working on this book. Thank you for making me laugh more than any other human ever could, for indulging me when I need a Bravo marathon or a nap in the sun, for being the greatest father and role model to our beautiful children, and for always putting our family first. I love you now and forever.

# About the Author

Denise Clifford is a professional organizer, a wife, a mom of two, a businesswoman with 20 years of experience, and has been helping organize homes for over 10 years. She holds a B.B.A. In Advertising from Pace University in New York City.

Clifford is a highly regarded authority on the subject of home organization. She has been a professional organizer for years, launching her own brand DeeCluttered in 2020. She is also a sought-after lifestyle expert for the media and has been quoted in MSN and Homes & Gardens, as well as other prestigious media outlets.

Clifford has helped transform the lives of countless families through her no-nonsense, uncomplicated, and direct but fun approach to getting organized. She is currently in development of a lifestyle home organization television program and a line of products, designed to help people gain back control of their space, their mind, and their lives.

She lives in NJ with her really handsome and intelligent husband and two extremely clever and talented children.

Join the conversation, share your frustrations, struggles or ask for advice on the areas of the home that are causing the most challenges for you by reaching out to Denise directly at denise@deecluttered.com or participate in the various polls and quizzes posed on her Instagram account @dee.cluttered. Tag your before and after pictures using **#igotdeecluttered** to be a part of the DeeCluttered community and be the first to know about giveaways or holiday discounts.

Printed by Amazon Italia Logistica S.r.l.
Torrazza Piemonte (TO), Italy

58407835R00107